PACIFIC NORTHWEST HAUNTS

A GHOST HUNTER'S FIELD GUIDE

JOE TEEPLES

Schiffer Publishing Ltd®

4880 Lower Valley Road, Atglen, Pennsylvania 19310

Copyright © 2010 by Joe Teeples
Unless otherwise noted, all photos are the property of the author.
Library of Congress Control Number: 2009942030

Designed by "Sue"
Type set in Demon Night/NewBskvll BT
ISBN: 978-0-7643-3436-8
Printed in the United States of America

CONTENTS

"At night, when the streets of your cities and villages shall be silent, and you think them deserted, they will throng with the returning hosts that once filled and still love this beautiful land."

-- Chief Seattle, 1854

Introduction

The Associated Press conducted a telephone poll in October 2007, interviewing over 1,000 people. Forty-eight percent of those surveyed said they believed in some form of ESP, nineteen percent believed in the existence of spells or witchcraft, fourteen percent believed in UFOs, and one in five said that they were superstitious.

Then the survey asked about ghosts. One-third of the respondents said they believed that those "bumps in the night" could be ghostly spirits. Three of every ten people have been wakened in the middle of the night and could sense a strange presence in the room with them. Almost one in four people claimed to have either felt the presence of a ghost or have seen one.

This phenomenon is not limited to the United States — foreign countries often report ghost stories with less "tongue in cheek" than the US press. For example, in late 2008 a headline from Kuala Lumpur in Malaysia reported that a burglar who had broken into a house claimed a spirit had held him captive for three days! Local newspeople treat ghost reports as more of a special interest topic. For example, when a pair of residents in Federal Way reported to the police that ghosts had repeatedly sexually assaulted them in their apartment, the matter was referred to Ross Allison of the local ghost-hunting organization, AGHOST, for investigation.

Paranormal research is based on finding facts that support theories. This research can be in the field of Extra Sensory Perception (ESP), hunting Sasquatch/Yeti, tracking UFOs, or exploring Life After Death experiences. Any study begins with a theory that researchers attempt to prove or disprove by collecting scientific facts using scientific equipment and techniques to explore the spiritual world. The scientific method requires that a scientist gather data using observation and experimentations to develop a hypothesis. This hypothesis would attempt to explain the phenomenon and allow researchers to build experiments on which to prove or disprove the hypothesis.

In order to find facts on ghosts, researchers need to know where various sightings or anomalies have taken place. That is the purpose of this book. This field manual is designed to give researchers an up-to-date account of reported hauntings, as well as their locations so that investigations can continue. These locations have been researched and substantiated. Street addresses for the locations have been included so that the reader can find the area using an Internet based driving system. A description of what has been reported and photographs have been provided as well. Spurious reports, such as "something weird happens at xxx location" have been omitted so that field researchers can focus on factual studies that can be verified.

Ghost hunters and other investigators of the paranormal have broken down the hauntings into separate categories. They are:

† The Holy Grail

To a ghost hunter, this is the full apparition... a spirit that has passed on, but can still be seen and is often mistaken for a living person. For example, a group of ghost hunters were in the cemetery overlooking Seattle on New Year's Eve (Great place to watch the fireworks) when a security guard from the homeless encampment next door came over and asked what they were doing. When they told them they were ghost hunters, the guard said, "Oh, looking for ghosts, huh?" Then he wandered away. When the team was done and were leaving the cemetery, they went to the encampment to thank the guard for looking in on them. They were told that there were no guards there, and that no one had gone over to "that spooky place."

Other apparitions include the attractive young lady who is seen at Andy's Diner and is pursued into the back rooms by staff members wanting to get her phone number... Or the woman at the Georgetown Castle that is so lifelike, artists have painted her portrait! Other ghosts seem to keep a form of their former shape, such as the "blue lady" of Skykomish who seems to glow with a blue radiance. Or the many spirits that are seen in theaters as smoke or fog.

† The Residual Ghost

This ghost does the same thing over and over and doesn't interact with any witnesses. Like a broken recording, the image repeats itself, such as the faded image of a woman climbing up a staircase that is no longer there. (See the Georgetown Castle)

† The Anniversary Ghost

This ghost causes things to occur on a specific date and tends to interact or try to communicate with the witness. The appearance of a girl at a local park on January 8th each year is an example. (See Des Moines Park)

† Intelligent or Active Ghosts

These ghosts have the ability to interact with witnesses, move items, and seem lifelike. Many people who encounter these specters don't realize it was a ghost until they are told later on that the person they claim to have seen has been dead for quite some time. (See the Blue Lady at Skykomish)

Ghosts don't seem to be concerned with years. In the first part of 1980, tales began to circulate around Southwestern Washington of a ghostly hitchhiker. Police departments received reports of a spectral woman who was spotted on Interstate 5 and local highways. The drivers were startled to see a woman wearing a white dress walking along the shoulder, signaling for a ride. When the driver stopped, she would crawl into the back seat and sit quietly for a while, and then she'd start to talk about Mount Saint Helens.

The woman would tell the driver that the mountain was going to erupt again, and then...she would vanish. Sometimes she would be specific and tell the drivers that the mountain would erupt on October 12th and 14th. When the time came and went, people laughed with relief; the sightings became less frequent and then stopped altogether. As if to demonstrate that years mean little to ghosts, scientists watched as St. Helens began to throw ash and steam into the atmosphere once again and molten lava punched through the surface again. The recorded date that the lava punched through the crater floor was...October 12, 2004.

This book is a comprehensive field guide for those who would like to investigate spirit sightings on the West Coast of the United States. It is not an attempt to prove or disprove that a location is haunted, but to provide factual reports of activity that may indicate the presence of some type of spirit. The reader is encouraged to develop one or two theories based on the events chronicled within these pages and then head out and test those theories.

For those who would like to take a ghost hunting trip up or down the West Coast, we have included sightings from Anchorage, Alaska to Portland, Oregon. The list is far from complete, but it provides a starting point for researchers. So grab your flashlight, camera, and tape recorder and head out on an adventure! Stay overnight in a haunted hotel, sign up to take a ghost tour, and visit a cemetery! If you keep your eyes open, I guarantee you'll see some strange and unusual things in this great land of ours. Let me know what you discover!

Section One:

HAUNTED LOCATIONS

Chapter One:

APPARITIONS OF ALASKA

While Alaska recently joined the United States, it has a long, vibrant history in a violent environment that lends itself to those events that tend to inspire ghostly stories. The Native Americans in that region have grown up with and cherish their heritage, which includes the recognition and understanding of the spirit world. With the arrival of "modern man" in the region, these forces have been known to interact and let themselves be known.

ANCHORAGE

Courtyard Hotel
4901 Spenard Street

Located near the Anchorage Airport, the Courtyard Hotel has a guest who won't check out...even in death. It has been reported that a man died in Room 201 several years ago. His body was not discovered for several days and, according to some researchers, he's still at the hotel, haunting Room 201. The ghostly spirit has been seen, but researchers have been unable to make direct contact or have conversations with him.

The Courtyard Hotel in Anchorage has a "guest" that won't check out!

Another ghost that walks around the parking lot and gazebo area of the hotel has been seen so often that employees call him "Ken."

A cat has been seen haunting the hotel as well. The feline seems to be particularly fond of rooms 103 and 107.

Anchorage Hotel
330 E Street

The downtown Anchorage area is proud of the oldest hotel in the city, the historic Anchorage Hotel, which is listed on the National Register of Historic places. Built in 1936 on the corner of 3rd Avenue and E Street, this was the only place in the new city where people could enjoy a meal served on fine china, complete with linen and silver.

Many guests have seen a ghostly girl on the second floor. Curtains rumble, shower curtains sway by themselves, and pictures have been known to fly through the air. The picture over the mantelpiece actually flew across the room and struck the coffee table! Many of these events have been attributed to "Black Jack" Sturgus, the city's first Police Chief who was found shot in the back from a bullet from his own gun, just a few steps from the hotel. It seems that his spirit returns to the scene of the crime annually, around February 20 (He died in 1921), seeking justice for the unsolved crime!

Hotel employees have reported hearing the sound of guests coming down the stairs, only to find that there is no one on the stairs. A spirit of a man has been seen at the base of the stairs walking around that same area. Others report seeing what they describe as an insane old woman and another spirit of a happy little boy, who seems to delight in running up and down the hall, disturbing guests who call the front desk to complain of noisy children, when none are even registered at the hotel!

Some of the rooms, such as 215 and 217, seem to have resident spirits that turn the televisions on and off. These spirits seem to enjoy cleanliness, as they often turn the bath water on and off as well.

One spirit was to be wed in 1920, but her fiancé made it in the gold rush and jilted her on her wedding day. She can sometimes be seen wailing in the halls of the hotel, still wearing the wedding dress that she hanged herself in on her wedding day so many years ago.

When visiting the historic Anchorage Hotel, ask to see the ghost log that the hotel keeps, where a number of guests have shared their encounters, along with evidence of several other spirits and former guests who have checked in...but never checked out!

SKAGWAY

Golden North Hotel
3rd Avenue and Broadway

Two ghosts haunt this hotel. Workers believe that one of the spirits is that of a young woman who died in her room of pneumonia. She was waiting for her fiancé to return from a gold-hunting expedition. Her spirit haunts Room 23…guests have reported seeing her. They also claim to have experienced the sensation of being choked — as if they had pneumonia themselves — in that room in the middle of the night.

A second spirit has been reported in Room 14… Here a strange "light form" has been seen that moves around the room at night.

VILLAGE OF ST. MARY

One of the native tribes near the Village of St. Mary in Alaska has a bunkhouse type of residence/dormitory/billets used for workers in the area. At 5:15 in the morning a man woke to see the vision of an old woman walking down the steps and out the door. She seemed to be talking to herself, saying, "not to sleep… not to sleep…"

At breakfast, the man asked if anyone else had seen the old woman in the bunkhouse. The tribal elders informed him of the story of an old man who got sick there ninety-three years ago. His wife was with him when he died and felt that if she could only keep awake he would recover. Her spirit has been seen ever since, roaming the halls and muttering to herself not to doze off. She has been seen frequently roaming the dormitory and walking around the billets. Others have heard doors closing and footsteps when no earthly presence is around.

Chapter Two:

PARANORMAL PORTLAND

The Shanghai Tunnels of Portland have a wicked and sordid past, very much like the Seattle Underground Tour passageways. These tunnels run beneath Portland and some pubs and taverns actually had trap doors that opened into this labyrinth. When sailors would have too much to drink, they would often fall through these trap doors to be seized upon by criminals below who would kidnap them, drug them, and sell them to ship masters who were sailing to oriental ports. This was a form of slavery at the turn-of-the-century that Portland residents recall with both pride and shame. The sailor would wake up at sea and have to work for his passage. As a result, the term "You've been Shanghaied" was born! Women were also kidnapped in the same way and sold into the sex trade.

THE HAUNTED HOTSPOTS

Bagdad Theater
3702 SE Hawthorne

One of many 1920s style theaters, the Bagdad was built to seat about seven hundred people and originally had a large balcony overlooking the auditorium. Recent owners have removed some of the front row seats to accommodate tables for patrons to place their food and drink while they enjoy the show.

When electricians were rewiring the theater in 1994, they turned off the main power to the lights. The lights went out normally and then they turned back on again, flickering off and on for about an hour. Finally, they stayed off while the electricians tried to figure out what had happened, to no avail.

Another witness was washing his hands in the second floor restroom when he felt a cold wind blow through the closed room. The wind blew the toilet paper on the rolls and the cloth towel on the circular towel rack was blown sideways.

Buttertoes Restaurant
1244 SE Belmont Street

Now a private residence, the old restaurant is haunted by a female ghost that has been seen at various times. The ghost has been named "Lydia" and she seems to enjoy revealing herself to those who don't believe in spirits. She wears a turn-of-the-century style high-top shirt. This may be the same Lydia who has been reported at Columbian Cemetery (old name was Love Cemetery).

The Comedy Sports Arena
1963 NW Kearney Street

Located in Northwest Portland between 19th Avenue and NW Kearney Street, this venue hosts improvisational comedy shows several times a week along the lines of "Who's Line is it, Anyway?" When the building is mostly empty, the few performers and employees left have heard a woman talking in the back room where the costumes and equipment are stored. When they check the area out, no one is there. This ghostly speech sometimes erupts into laughter and increases in volume. Still, no one is there.

Lights have been seen in parts of the building and, when the workers go back to turn them off, they found that no lights were on in the darkened area. In the ladies' room, the toilet has had a tendency to flush itself endlessly with no explanation. It seems that this female ghostly entity loves to play with the water and finds the costumes amusing!

Fairmount Apartments
NW 26th Avenue and Vaughn Streets

Formerly a grand hotel, this apartment building was used in the 1905 Lewis and Clark Expedition celebration. It is the final building still standing from that time. Over the years, residents have seen apparitions late at night roaming the building. There are ghosts on all floors of this structure. The ghosts that reside in the lower floors seem to be more hostile than those on the upper floors.

Hollywood Theater
NE Sandy Boulevard and 41st Street

At this theater, which has been around since the 1920s, ghosts rattle pipes backstage on a regular basis. No less than four managers have reported seeing a ghost. The spirit is that of a man in a white suit in the upstairs lobby.

At the Hollywood Theater, a ghost has been seen in the upstairs lobby.

Hallock Modey Advertising Firm
2445 NW Irving Street

People have heard footsteps in the halls when they work alone at the agency, and the smell of lavender will sometimes permeate the room when no one is around. Apparitions have been seen ascending the main stairwell on the inside of the building. The sound of an older, crotchety woman's spirit has been heard to say, "Stop it."

One day, when a woman was working alone in the agency, she needed a piece of black paper. Not being able to find one, she said aloud in the empty office, "We're an ad agency and we don't have a piece of black paper?" Behind her — *in the still empty office* — the copy machine sprang to life and produced one sheet of blackened paper to the amazement of the woman.

Hoodoo Antiques
122 NW Couch Street

The objects at this antiques store seem to be haunted and have a life of their own. Alarms go off by themselves while pictures, as well as other items, seem to be moved by invisible hands.

Some say that the basement is haunted, where merchandise move about on its own or is replaced. Some workers complain of an odd feeling downstairs and blame it on the ghost that dwells there. They refuse to go in the basement.

At Hoodoo Antiques, things move on their own in the basement.

Imperial Arms Apartments
1429 SW 14th Avenue

This five-story brick building was erected in the 1900s near Portland State University and the Northwest Culinary Institute. Entrance is gained through a front courtyard with beautiful landscaping and Old World charm that extends to the common areas of the apartments.

Through the years, residents have reported apparitions in the building. One is an older man who has been observed in the basement of the apartments. Some think that this is the spirit of one of the managers of the building from the past who refuses to move on. Another apparition has been seen on the second floor of the building. This ghost is a young man who is wearing clothes that seem to date to the 1970s.

Residents have reported closet doors slamming, cold spots in the apartments, and voices when no one is about. In one case, some type of ooze or ectoplasm was found on a pair of shoes.

Joe's Cellar
1332 NW 21st Avenue

This building was the site of an old brothel at the turn-of-the-century. It is now a popular coffee shop, but in the old days gambling and prostitution took place. Some say that the Shanghai Tunnels are beneath the back parking lot and that some of the tunnel's openings can be found in the basement. The upstairs of the building has no electricity and is used for storage.

Ghosts here are known to move objects, causing them to vanish and then re-appear in out-of-the-way places. When the bar is empty, voices can be heard. Employees have seen the full apparition of a woman looking at them from the upstairs window onto the parking lot; they have nicknamed the spirit "Tess."

Ghost hunters feel that there are several ghosts in this place. One is that of a prostitute who died in a fire, a man who seems to be mentally challenged, and a little "wiener dog" that has a collar that jingles. Several employees have seen the dog yipping and running through the bar, but when they give chase, the animal vanishes!

The investigators have also picked up male and female voices as electronic voice phenomenon (EVPs). The female voice speaks briefly and in quick sentences. While the fire alarm has been disconnected, EVP sounds record that of a fire alarm going off!

Lotus Nightclub
932 SW 3rd Avenue

This card room and café is in the downtown area of Portland. Some employees have been spooked by something in the basement, and few are willing to reveal their experiences. One bartender went into the basement and heard a CO_2 canister release some gas. When he went back upstairs, he found an upside down shot glass on the bar that he had just cleared off before going downstairs.

Mama Mia's Tratoria Pizza
439 SW Second Avenue

This Italian restaurant sits over the connection point of five of the Shanghai Tunnels where ghosts have been reported. Opium was sold in the back of the building in the late 1800s. The owner has tried to rid the property of evil spirits, perhaps to cleanse the area of one of the suicides that took place in the basement. One ghost seems to be that of a woman and the other is that of a man. It seems that the male spirit is more of a controlling type.

Mama Mia's has a controlling male ghost... The ghost of a woman has also been seen there.

Old Town Pizza is haunted by the spirit of a brothel worker, Nina, who will vanish if you look directly at her.

Old Town Pizza Company
226 NW Davis Street

Visitors to this restaurant have noticed that the cage where you order your pizza is the original reception desk of Merchants Hotel. Beneath the pizza tavern, the Shanghai Tunnels connect Portland through dark underground pathways that were used to nab sailors and bring them to waiting ships docked on the river. Customers can order their own spirits at the bar as well. Try their house special…it's to die for! Many guests grab a copy of their take-out menu as a souvenir of their visit. It has a synopsis of their haunted connection with the city on the back.

The basement is haunted by the ghost of one of the prostitutes who was murdered here and still wanders the hundred-year-old building and nearby tunnels. Some say that a woman, who goes by the name of Nina, was sold into white slavery to be a prostitute. Nina (pronounced "Nigh-na") is a constant presence at the restaurant.

Traveling missionaries learned of Nina's fate and convinced the young woman to share information about her existence in exchange for her being freed. She cooperated, but was soon found dead in the hotel, having been thrown down the elevator shaft. She has been seen on the balcony watching guests as well as wandering the basement. Somewhere along the line, the name "NINA" was carved into the brick in one of the passageways in the tunnel. Visitors have reported that the spectral image of Nina tends to keep close to that area. Patrons have felt her presence, the faint smell of her perfume, and have even spotted her in her black dress wandering in the basement or simply observing the guests!

Pittock Mansion
3229 NW Pittock Drive

Purchased by the city in 1964, the house has been open to the public since 1965. Since that time, the framed picture of Henry Pittock as a boy has been kept on the bedroom mantle. Minutes after seeing it, tour guides have found that the picture has moved to a different location without the aid of a living person.

Some people have also reported seeing an older female spirit standing in the house; "she" vanishes when they look directly at her. Tourists have reported the aroma of flowering roses when no roses are in the house; tour guides have said that Georgianna Pittock loved roses and that she lived in the house until her death in 1918. Some people have heard the sound of heavy footsteps or boots walking in or out of the rear entrance of the home.

University of Portland
5000 North Willamette Road

At the University of Portland's Franz Hall, a janitor was on the second floor cleaning when he said that all of the mechanical doors locked on him. These doors can only be opened and closed by pushing a master button. Fortunately, the janitor had the keys to the lock box on the wall that controls the doors.

In the theater, the spirit of a young girl dressed in Victorian clothing has been spotted in the storage area in the basement and in the draft room late at night. She has been seen wearing a dress from the 1900s and sometimes with a hat that has lace trim on it. She has also been seen on the stage. Students report that she tries to touch them and has been known to change the station of their radio if she doesn't like the song.

In Waldschmidt Hall, students have reported hearing the footsteps of an invisible entity following them. They also say that there are dark figures that seem to hide in the corners.

Villa St. Rose School
597 North Dekum Street

The Villa St. Rose School for girls in North Portland has gone by many names. Most recently it has been known as the Rosemont Commons Development. The Villa St. Rose Convent began at that location and can still be seen in the new development, which retained the structure for rehabilitation. The building is listed in the National Register of Historic Places and has been a neighborhood landmark since the 1900s.

The Sisters of the Good Shepherd ran the Villa as a convent and a school for young women. With expenses increasing and the number of

At Villa St. Rose, listen for the laughter of spectral children.

nuns available to operate the school diminishing, the school was closed. It opened later in 1980 as the Rosemont School for Girls. It was vacated around 1995 when the girls' school moved to Southeast Portland. The site was vacant, standing as an open invitation for vandalism, until it was re-developed as the Rosemont Commons. People have said that in the old gym, they can hear the laughter and voices of spectral children, plus their little feet running around.

White Eagle Tavern
835 North Russell Street

One of the McMenamins Pubs, this tavern has been a local watering hole since 1905. Patrons could partake of the upstairs brothel or enjoy the opium den that was downstairs. It seems that there was a "white" brothel upstairs and a "colored" brothel in the basement. There was also a tunnel that connected the place to the infamous Shanghai Tunnels that led to the waterfront. A prostitute named Rose was killed in the upstairs brothel by a jealous lover in 1926.

More recently a waitress was half pushed and half carried down the basement steps by a firm, invisible force. Psychics claim to sense a feeling of sadness coming from the second floor, and in the basement get a feeling of death and violence. Room #2 is said to be haunted by a Polish man called Sam. Witnesses report strange sounds in the building, including footsteps in empty corridors, doors unlocking by themselves, toilets flushing by themselves, and toilet paper rolls flying from one stall to another!

Employees have smelled smoke when there is no fire in the area. At other times, they can smell the odor of cheap perfume. In the kitchen area off of the office area, there is a stairway that is said to be haunted. One manager was trapped in there by cleaning equipment, or so they say! The spirits seem to enjoy touching or pushing people...patrons say that invisible hands have grabbed them.

Yellowbrick Road Antique Shop
5916 SE 91st Avenue

A spirit resides at this shop...one that has been known to play pranks on people and make noises that can be heard in or through the walls. It has even been known to push people.

Yur's Restaurant and Lounge
717 NW 16th Avenue

Shadowy figures are often reported here out of the corner of the eye, but when one looks directly at them, they disappear. Employees have reported cold spots at various areas around the building and some say that they have seen a man's face in a corner of the restaurant.

GHOSTS IN THE PARKS

Willamette River
A rowboat is said to haunt this river. Every once in a while this empty rowboat is sighted moving along the river. Spectators call the Coast Guard who heads out to retrieve it. When the Coast Guard gets close to the boat, it...vanishes before their eyes!

Scapponia Park
In North Portland's Scapponia Park, history buffs will tell you that in the 1800s a horse thief lived in an old cabin in this area. One night an angry mob descended on the criminal and shot his dog. Then they hanged the man and buried both him and his dog beneath a large oak tree that can be found in the campground. Some say that they still see the old man and his dog wandering around the park to this day.

Tryon Creek State Park

Located at 11321 SW Terwilliger Road, this was once lumber country, where sites of horse-drawn sleighs were common. Down by the creek, visitors report hearing the sounds of ghostly men preparing for their day of work in the lumber trade. Along the North Rim Trail, people claim to have heard the sound of horses in harnesses hauling timber and even the smell of fresh cut timber.

Cathedral Park

In 1949, a young fifteen-year-old girl named Thelma Taylor was kid-napped, bound, and raped under the St. Johns Bridge in Cathedral Park. It is said that she was held prisoner at that location for a week before finally passing away. Portland police have responded to calls about the sound of screams coming from that area of the park when no one is around.

Chapter Three:

SUPERNATURAL SEATTLE

Seattle is rich in a history that celebrates the coming together of people from around the world in a colorful mosaic of life. Visitors to the Emerald City are fascinated by the art and various wonders that abound. Seattle's communities reflect the ethnicity, traditions, and values of the settlers who sought to make a lasting impression in the city. Today tourists visit the remains of the World Fair and ride the monorail to a thriving shopping district to enjoy a cup of Starbucks coffee. Other visitors explore Pike Market, with its beautiful flower vendors, fruit stands, and fish markets. One may even see the famous flying fish zooming over the heads of tourists. Across the street from the market are bakeries and pubs that beg to be explored.

Like most major cities, Seattle has a dark side. The city has not embraced its racy past as some municipalities have. The colorful stories of murder and mayhem rival those of Chicago, Detroit, or New York City. Like Chicago, Seattle had its own version of the great fire that leveled the city and has had its historic share of graft, corruption, kidnapping, and murder.

Most Americans are familiar with the terms "skid row" and "graveyard shift." However, few realize that the terms originated in Seattle. Skid Row was used to describe the treacherous and wet road used to bring lumber to a steam-powered sawmill in early Seattle. This road is now called Yesler Street in memory of Mr. Yesler, who helped establish the city and provided the first steam-powered sawmill in the area.

The names of the city founders are found on the streets as well as in the cemeteries. Mercer, Denny, Yesler, Magnusson, Renton, and Holgate were all founders of this thriving metropolis and their names are now heard in the local traffic reports each morning. There is more to these people who lived fascinating lives in this new land than just a slab of asphalt or a chunk of concrete. If only they could reach across the years and speak to us... It would appear that some of them are trying to do just that. While exploring Seattle's spirited past, visitors might find themselves in the following areas:

**The Waterfront ~ Pike Market ~ Belltown ~
Pioneer Square ~ Capitol Hill ~ University District
~ Georgetown ~ Metropolitan Seattle**

The Waterfront

Home of piers, ports, and curiosity shops

Waterfront Marriott
2100 Alaskan Way

When the hotel was being built, they found a pylon with a chain on it that they could not move, so they built around it. The hotel has problems with sewage seeping into the basement and unexplained smells. Reportedly this was all Indian land long ago and the original occupants of the land may be making their presence known!

Ye Olde Curiosity Shop
1001 Alaskan Way

This shop on Alaskan Way is on the waterfront itself. Inside the shop are rare artifacts and unusual offerings that attract tourists throughout the year. Toward the back of the store are the mummified remains of people

Ye Olde Curiosity Shop has plenty of ghosts in the back of its store.

and animals. This is the area where most of the unusual events have occurred, including things moving by themselves, temperature changes, and lights going on and off with no human intervention. The shop's sister store, Ye Olde Curiosity Shoppe Too, is supposedly haunted by the spirit of a sailor.

OK Hotel
212 Alaskan Way

The OK Hotel was built in 1917 as a low-income hotel with 192 rooms. Currently housing art galleries, the hotel is open to the public during the Art Walk on the first Thursday of each month at 6 p.m. It was featured as the central coffee shop in the 1992 Warner Bros. movie "Singles," which also featured a scene of Jimmi Hendrix's grave at Renton Cemetery.

The hotel was originally located under the viaduct in Pioneer Square and hosted musical acts in the bar until the Nisqually earthquake struck on February 28, 2001. The entire region suffered extensive damage during that event. The ghosts seem to be located in the upper floors of that building. As far back as 1933, the spirit of a Native American has been seen at the hotel.

Pier 70

On the water's edge, near the Victoria Clipper's berth, this pier is the site where locals have reported a clipper ship that appears mysteriously out of a highly localized fog bank or mist. The ship and its young captain only seem to be visible to those who are in the throes of despair, with the captain speaking to them and encouraging them to persevere in their struggles. He assures them that their fortunes will indeed improve. In truth, those witnesses who have spoken with the captain have seen their lives improve. The image appears solid and lifelike to the persons who are able to see him, but remain invisible to everyone else!

PIKE MARKET (1508 PIKE PLACE)

> **Famous for an American Indian Princess that haunts the halls...and vanishes before visitors' eyes.**

Built on a site that was sacred to local Indians, in 1907 Pike Market was established as a farmers' market serving Seattle with a wide variety of services, from fruits and vegetables, to meat, to haircuts at the Barber Shop, where a very fat female barber used to lull her clients to sleep by singing

Pike Market is full of ghosts and hosts a ghost tour!

soft lullabies to them in the 1950s. Once her customers were asleep, she would go through their pockets and rob them. She died when the floor gave way beneath her and she fell through. Some people at the market have claimed to hear her ghost trying to lull them to sleep.

For generations Pike Market has been a place where people gathered to trade stories, tales, goods, and services. Since the legend claims it was originally sacred Indian land, to commemorate this sacred meeting place, a piece of art called "A Point" was dedicated in 1992 at the Spirit Meeting Place on Western Avenue towards the back of the Market. Janitors cleaning the lower levels of the market report hearing singing near this area after hours. The tip of the artwork is designed to be a focal point for those who communicate with the spirits. This sculpture is in an alcove at the base of the stairs leading to the market, near the sky bridge. Look for the 1992 plaque that commemorates the area in memory of Michael Oren.

Guided tours of Pike Market, lasting about an hour, are available. The tours cost $10 to $12 dollars and are conducted by Michael Yaeger, who may be contacted at Studio Solstone (206-624-9102 or 206-682-7453). Sheila Lyon of the Pike Place Magic Shop also conducts ghostly tours and she can be reached at 206-713-8506.

Haunts at the Market

There are numerous ghosts haunting the place, as footsteps of phantoms can be heard in areas that are known to be unoccupied. They include an old Native American woman, a young boy, and an African American man.

Native American Woman Ghost

The ghost of a Native American woman has been seen in the market at night when all the tourists and shoppers have gone home. The spirit moves slowly and people have said that she changes her appearance from glowing white to pink and then to blue. She is supposed to be Princess Angelina, the daughter of Chief Sealth. She is often seen in the Down Under area of the market, even though she was physically laid to rest in Lakeview Cemetery. She is sometimes referred to as the 'White Lady' and her eyes are reported to be a very bright blue. Sometimes she is seen accompanied by a young boy.

At Cutters Bayhouse Restaurant, located near Pike Market (2001 Western Avenue), when the wait staff drops something such as a plate or coffee cup, a scowling Princess Angelina is sometimes seen at the kitchen door. During one wedding party, the Princess made her appearance in front of seventeen guests. When the father of the bride demanded to know who had invited this disheveled spirit by announcing "who let this homeless person in?"…she disappeared. Some people at the restaurant say that they have seen a woman wearing a black dress approach them. The woman has no face and in a short time disappears.

The Boy Ghost

A ghost of a child is known to haunt the Bead Emporium (Bead Zone). This shop is located in the area known as the "Market Down Under," near the area where the old horse stables were. When renovations were done to this business a few years ago, a basket of beads was discovered within the wall…an improbability since there was no access for this space, as the door had been painted shut years before the store opened. Thread has also been unraveled and beads are sometimes thrown at customers. Beads have fallen off their hooks, and objects seem to find their way to new spots during this childlike, mischievous haunting.

The ghostly child seems to enjoy playing with the cash register, and a new puppet shop seems to have attracted his attention as he seems to visit the marionettes in the evening. This may be the spirit of "Jacob," the son of Polish immigrants who enjoys mixing his favorite red beads into boxes of other colors of beads. Jacob worked as a groom in the stable in the early days and was known to pick pockets from time to time to buy treats, but was a popular sight at the market with a wonderful smile, crooked teeth and all. Jacob passed away from pneumonia or some other lung infection.

The Crystal Ball

In the early days of the market, Madam Nora presided over the Temple of Destiny. She practiced the art of Egyptian sand divination at stall #14 in the lower market. This prophetess would practice crystal gazing, an Indian psychic projection. Someone brought a crystal ball to the Pharaohs Treasure and wanted to trade the crystal in exchange for something else. The seller did not take money, mumbling something about a strange market woman who lived inside the crystal ball. The ball sat among scarabs in this Egyptian shop and the owners reported that sometimes they found things had moved around during the night.

The crystal eventually found its way to the Pike Place Magic Shop. There, it was on display for years, with numerous bothersome events attributed to it. These pesky events persisted and eventually became too much for even a magic shop to handle, so the owner removed the crystal ball from display. The magic shop has friendly people working there who will provide help to those seeking ghosts in the market. They sell a ghost-hunting guide that is kept behind the counter and is available for those who ask for it.

The Dancing Ghost

During the Second World War, employees of Boeing Airplane Company used Pike Market as a place to hold dances. After they finished their swing shift at the plant, workers would arrive at the market to relax and seek someone to dance with. Female workers filled the role of "Rosie the Riveter" for the war effort and helped produce the airplanes that won the war. They eagerly sought the company of a handsome young man who was a fantastic dancer. He was light on his feet, very polite, and always entertained the ladies as a complete gentleman. The only problem was that he was a spirit. The ladies would dance with him and he would eventually disappear into the evening. His spirit lives on and this dapper ghost can sometimes be seen on the upper floors of the market.

Shopping Around for a Ghost

Pike Market actually consists of a series of buildings constructed on the old property. While most visitors tend to consider the main building the prime attraction, there are other ghostly occurrences at the shops and buildings considered to be a part of the Pike Market complex.

Down Under Bookstore

At Shakespeare's Books (Down Under Bookstore), the same book was found on the floor at opening time by the owner's mother. The book would be dusted off and replaced on the shelves, only to be found on the floor the next morning. The book was eventually destroyed. A few years later an author wrote a story while sitting at a desk in the same place where the book was always found on the floor. She did not know about the ghostly book...yet in the beginning of the book she describes the same ghost in the bookstore.

Goodwin Library

Frank Goodwin was a real estate developer who built much of the early market. As director of the Market, he managed it from 1918 to 1941 from his upper level office, which is now Goodwin Library. There are reports that he frequents the site of his office at times. People have reported seeing an image looking down at them; sometimes the image is seen swinging a golf club. Others have seen the figure of a tall imposing gentleman strolling in Post Alley at night, dressed in a top hat and black suit carrying a cane.

Mr. D's Greek Deli

There are fighting spirits in the meat locker of this restaurant located in the triangle building next to Post Alley. Mr. D is an artist who sculpts with meat and stores his work of celebrity busts in the walk-in freezer located downstairs. The spirits seem to take turns slicing off noses and ears of his meat sculptures. Workers do not like going down there to confront the battling ghosts that fight each other on a regular basis.

Kells Irish Pub

Located at 1916 Post Alley, this pub is considered part of the Pike Place Market district. It used to be the embalming room for one of Seattle's oldest mortuaries, ER Butterworth. The bodies were prepared for display at Kells and then moved to the chapel at 1st Street and Virginia Avenue in Belltown. If you look up at the third floor, you can still see the painted letters of "Butterworth" on the cement.

People have reported strange sightings of a little girl and candles have been known to light themselves in this bar.

The ghostly girl seems to enjoy playing with living little girls when there is a function or party at the pub. Children often tell their parents that they were playing with a little girl who lives at the pub, but when the

Above Kells Tavern is the sign for the old ER Butterworth's Mortuary!

parents try to locate the little girl, she has vanished from the back of the bar room.

Kells is a nice Irish pub that should be explored with a pint of Guinness...or some other spirit.

Alibi Room

At this restaurant, located just off Post Alley, people report meeting a ghost known as Frank. They know it is Frank since this elderly ghost has been known to introduce himself by name to people outside the restrooms!

The kitchen of the Alibi Room used to be the living quarters for a German or Russian immigrant worker who was a maid in the Market hotel. She worked there in exchange for room and board and led a short, unhappy life. She spoke no English and had no friends. She seemed to enjoy watching the glamorous dancers and prostitutes who frequented the Market, but knew that she could never join them, adding to her loneliness. People have felt an immense sadness in the kitchen area, as they detect her presence, while others have reported smelling the strong, almost overpowering scent of "old ladies" perfume in the back of the market theater.

Pike Market Child Care and Preschool

An old children's clinic once operated at the site of the current Pike Market Child Care and Preschool. Spirit children seem to roam the area within the walls of the school. One ghostly boy in particular has short dark hair and wears a blue shirt. This elusive waif has been known to quickly dart behind objects, such as easels, and then vanish. Many workers have reported seeing the lad, but none have ever seen his face.

BELLTOWN

**Home of many pubs and other spirits
that haunt the lively clubs**

Butterworth's Mortuary
1921 First Avenue

Built in 1903 as ER Butterworth's Mortuary, this building houses several odd apparitions and was noted for poltergeist activity. It is located between Stewart and Virginia streets. In 1997, it was known as Café Sofie and went out of business. From 1997 to 2002, it was known as Avenue One...and went out of business. Then for a time it was known as a club called Fire and Ice, and in 2007, the Starlite Lounge died there. A Hawaiian Shaman visited the place and reported that he could see eighteen good spirits and

This restaurant is so haunted it can't keep its doors open! The bodies of the deceased used to be carted up from below to be viewed at this location!

one dark presence. The men's room is where the mortuary elevator shaft used to be...rumor has it that someone fell down it years ago.

John David Crow reported that he spent a few nights there in the late 1990s when it was the Avenue One pub. One morning he went to the bathroom to find a hanger perfectly balanced on the doorknob. As he watched it, the hanger fell off, but he has no idea how it got there in the first place.

Others claim that the spirits are some of the deceased who seem to be thin and emaciated. There was a time in Seattle when a local physician would attempt to starve illness out of patients by putting them on a tomato broth diet. Not only did it not cure the illness, the patients often died. They were then processed through this building!

The tiles in front of the building betray its former use as a mortuary!

One bartender told of hearing voices that "burble" late at night, as if a radio dial was being switched to different frequencies. One night a big customer broke into tears and rushed out of the restaurant after seeing a woman clutching a shawl staring at him from the hallway. It seems that she glided away without using her legs and blinked when she vanished. In one episode, two wine bottles flew off the wine rack and just missed striking the manager in the head. A vase that had been missing for some time appeared on a window table that had just been set. One diner fled the restaurant after he saw an old woman who seemed to be hugging a shawl disappear into a wall.

In 2006, the club took on the name "Starlite Lounge" after being redecorated. During the renovation, construction workers complained of people who would sit in the booths and criticize their work—and then vanish! One ghostly old gentleman told a worker that he was doing the job wrong and then, true to form, vanished. It is an active ghost haunt where investigators have reported over a dozen different spirits and floating balls of light. The entranceway still tells of the building's former use with tiles that spell out "Office" and "Chapel."

One table was called "the haunted booth" by management since some loyal customers always felt something strange when they sat there. One night the occupants of the booth taunted the ghost to try to get it to appear. A large chunk of ceiling plaster fell to the floor about five feet from the booth. A woman saw a pair of shoes in the bathroom stall, and as she watched, the shoes vanished into thin air!

The New Baker House
2327 1st Avenue

In 1921, this apartment complex was owned by 68-year-old Kate Mooers, who was also part owner of the Sophie Apartments at 409 Denny Way, where she lived. Kate wore expensive jewelry and drove a fancy sedan, but was known for being a miser. This didn't keep 37-year-old gold-digger James Mahoney from marrying her. James grew tired of the financial control that Kate placed him under.

James told friends and neighbors that he and Kate were going on a trip. When he showed up in Seattle eleven days later and started cashing American Express checks with Kate's forged signature, the authorities became suspicious. James had rented a houseboat at 1415 East Northlake Avenue and a small rowboat. He hired the Seattle Transfer Company to move a heavy trunk from the Sophia apartment on Denny Way to the houseboat on Lake Union.

It turns out that within a year of their wedding James had killed Kate in their Denny Way apartment, stuffed her — still breathing and alive — in a steamer trunk, covered her living body with quicklime, and tossed her body in Lake Union, east of the University Bridge. He was arrested for his crime and some feel that Kate is still haunts her old apartment.

Cherry Street Coffee Lounge
2721 1st Avenue

Located at the corner of First Avenue and Clay Street, this twelve-story building has shops on the ground floor and apartments above. Originally the city morgue for Seattle, it's now the home of the Cherry Street Coffee Lounge. This restaurant is on a prime corner and was an upscale steak house, then a Fine French Bistro, and then a Thai Restaurant.

Diners may not realize that they are sitting in the former chapel of one of Seattle's early mortuaries. Perhaps that is one reason why so many businesses come and go on this corner. The corner of Broad and First has a spectacular view of the space needle that seems to pop out of nowhere and should not be missed by tourists.

The Josephinium
1902 Second Avenue

Located near Stewart Street, this building was a grand ornate hotel built in 1902. Later it was used as a home for aged women in the 1960s. This fourteen-floor building is now owned by the Catholic Church and used to house elderly people. Said to be filled with ghosts, many residents claim to have witnessed ghosts wandering the building, but are reluctant to discuss it. However, when they do, the residents most often talk about "the woman on the stairs." One resident claims that the spirits "jump and they jump," but that she successfully used the power of prayer to keep them away from her apartment.

The Josephenium houses spirits that guard over the current residents.

Moore Theatre
1932 Second Avenue

Built in 1907 at Virginia and Second streets, this theater was Seattle's first vaudeville theater and looks as if it should be haunted. It probably is. During its heyday, it hosted such talent as Sarah Bernhard, Lily Langtry, and Marilyn Monroe. It was built with pomp and circumstance and cost between $350,000 and $500,000. This ornate theater was said to be the third largest in the country when it opened in December 1907 to a throng of 3,000 people! The social climate of the time even afforded a small gallery that could be accessed only from the street via an outside stairway, thus avoiding the lobby and mezzanine. This "separate but equal" gallery was reserved for Seattle's black audiences; however, it was removed long ago. The Moore Theater was placed on the National Register of Historic Places in 1974.

There is a female ghost haunting Moore Theater that seems to respond to the name "Abigail." It is interesting to note that the women's suffrage movement was active in Seattle and attracted such leading characters as Martha Landres (another Seattle ghost), Susan B. Anthony, and a suffragette from Oregon known as Abigail Duniway.

Dan Ireland and Darryl MacDonald owned the theater in the 1970s. They called it the Moore-Egyptian and lived in the dressing rooms beneath the building. One night in 1976 they returned home at 2 a.m. and Dan went to the projection booth to turn off the amplifier. When he got to the top of the darkened stairs, he heard a sighing sound and a bad smell resembling that of urine. He felt a cold tingling sensation and locked himself in the booth until Darryl came up. One employee said he felt like something was following him and then it "ran through" him. Employees at the theater attempted to have a séance after hours until they were discovered by Dan, who fired them.

Other incidents involved actors who had locked their dressing rooms on the top floor and found that someone had taken their shoes and placed them outside the door. There is rumored to be a ghost that cruises around the theater house and haunts the second jump, which is at the top of a fifty-foot ladder that reaches into the highest parts of the theater. More recently it has been reported that a man died from falling into the orchestra pit.

Opposite page:
Moore Theatre is one of the more haunted spots in Seattle.

Moore Hotel
1926 Second Avenue

This nearby hotel is located two blocks from Pike Market in the middle of Seattle's ride-the-bus-for-free zone. The city does not charge for bus rides on its transportation system within the downtown shopping district. The hotel is reported to be haunted by a little boy who drowned in the basement swimming pool. The pool has since been emptied of water and used as a storage area for years.

Moore Hotel... A young boy drowned in a swimming pool here, but has never left.

Rivoli Apartments
2127 Second Avenue

This turn-of-the-century building is home of the Trundle Bed ghost…a specter believed to be the spirit of an Eskimo girl who came to Seattle to start a new life in the 1980s. Her mentally ill Cuban boyfriend stabbed her to death and her body was hidden behind a Murphy bed. The door to her apartment was padlocked, so she wasn't discovered for several weeks until her neighbor noticed a strange smell.

The ghost of Christine, a former resident who used to clog her toilet to get attention, is said to also still be taking up residence there. While she was living, social workers tried to get her to move to a permanent hospital, but she refused and fought to stay at the Rivoli, a place she had grown to love. Christine's ghost has been sensed and felt by various tenants.

Two residents who died of AIDS are said to be standing guard over those who reside there. There was a shrine or memorial to the pair for a long time on the third floor of the building that they loved.

At the Rivoli, a man killed his girlfriend and hid her in a Murphy Bed until the neighbors complained of the smell!

Spitfire Lounge
2219 Fourth Avenue

Located between Bell and Blanchard streets, this club was formerly known as the Sit-n-Spin Laundromat. Before that, the story goes that Victor Meyers owned the building and called it Club Victor in 1932. This flamboyant man was the band leader in this club, which was the most popular hotspot in Seattle. After having run-ins with prohibition agents, he decided to run for Mayor of Seattle on a lark. He dressed up like Mahatma Ghandi and led a goat up Fourth Avenue to announce his candidacy. While he lost the race for Mayor, he later became Lieutenant Governor. Victor was called "The Clown Prince of Politics" and "The Pagliacci of Politics" in his heyday.

When the back room was first opened, the owner saw a silhouette of a man in a Fedora style hat on the back wall where a stage used to be. Psychics have felt things that coincide with the spirit on the wall.

In the 1990s, Lisa Bonney opened a club called the Sit-n-Spin at this location. An unknown ghost hunter offered to chase out the spirits for $200, but she refused. When the jukebox at the "Sit-n-Spin" was set on random mode, the music would always be the kind of jazz that was played in the 1930s at this location. Sometimes the iced tea machine would turn itself on and make a pot of tea all by itself. Employees have seen a headless apparition and one entertainer saw a man wearing an old-fashioned hat on the stage with her out of the corner of her eye. When she turned to face the spirit, it vanished. The spectators, though, hadn't seen anything. The ghost that haunts the club is said to be that of Vic Meyers.

Crocodile Café
2200 2nd Avenue

Located at the corner of Second Avenue and Blanchard Street, strange sightings and ghostly occurrences have been reported in this small theater that was the star of Seattle's vibrant music scene. It hosted such acts as Nirvana in 1992, Yoko Ono in 1996, Pearl Jam in 1997, and the Beastie Boys in 2007. In December of that year, it was forced to close its doors for financial reasons.

The Crocodile Café has hosted many musicians, including Nirvana and Yoko Ono. It also hosts many ghosts!

Lava Lounge
2226 Second Avenue

Located near Second Avenue and Bell Street, this lounge was an old seafarer's bar that later became known as Hawaii West. Customers report sounds of unearthly visitors from time to time. One manager reported hearing strange goings-on, which others had also experienced. She said that when she was alone she would hear things that would make her run.

Be ready to hear strange noises at the Lava Lounge.

The Rendezvous Lounge
2320 Second Avenue

Located near Battery Street and Second Avenue, this building was built in 1922 and held a speakeasy in the basement and an MGM movie house. Movies were shown at the Jewel Box Theater, where a ghost is said to occupy the projection booth just above the door to the theater.

When new owner Jerry Everand remodeled the building, there was a fire just after the kitchen re-opened. The only things that were burned were the parts left over from the 1920s. Nothing from the 1950s was damaged during this strange fire.

Customers have reported seeing a card dealer lurking around the place on Friday and Saturday nights. This suspicious character may be the 1930s comedian Jimmy Durante, who was the only person ever busted for dealing cards in the club.

The Rendezvous has a ghost in the projection booth and a spirited card dealer!

Hotel André
2000 4th Avenue

Known as the Claremont until 2004, this hotel is located at 4th Avenue and Virginia Street, kitty corner from the Bed Bath and Beyond store, lending new meaning to the term beyond. Employees have reported sounds of a violent, riotous party from the 1920s and the Prohibition era, complete with period jazz music and the sounds of breaking glass. In the 1960s, a worker is reported to have fallen to her death from the upper floors, possibly adding to the ghostly atmosphere of the place.

Visitors and staff have experienced levitating objects, such as a paperweight that dropped down onto a glass-covered desk making a loud noise, and one couple saw an apparition of a woman appear in their hotel room. The staff has become aware of the manifestations and complaints about the noise are common among hotel guests. When staff members go to investigate the disturbances, which seem to come largely from the ninth floor, the noise abruptly stops, only to start up again later.

The Hotel Andre doesn't like to talk about the noisy ghosts that levitate objects and appear and disappear at will!

Warwick Hotel
401 Lenora Street

This elegant hotel is one of Seattle's sophisticated downtown hotels… with a hidden history that they don't advertise. Management won't discuss it, but the bell hops and employees know that the place has spirits within its walls.

According to a local bell captain who used to work at this hotel, paranormal activity is in abundance and include sounds in the hallways and elevators running by themselves, as well as the usual kinds of spirited occurrences.

PIONEER SQUARE

The original city, razed by fire and rebuilt by pioneers, is home to Skid Row and was a departure point for many "Shanghaied" sailors!

Pioneer Square was Seattle's first neighborhood and laid the foundation for the rest of the city. Early Pioneer Square, it seems, was built on tidal flats that were regularly flooded with seawater, creating a quagmire in which horses and even children sank to their demise. It was in front of the Doc Maynard place that Chief Seattle addressed Governor Stevens who had been chosen as commissioner of Indian Affairs for the Washington Territory in 1854. Chief Seattle's words seem prophetic to ghost hunters as he explained that the commissioner should treat the Indians well. As Chief Seattle said:

> "And when the last red man shall have perished from the earth and his memory among white men shall have become a myth, these shores shall swarm with the invisible dead of my tribe, and when your children's children shall think themselves alone in the field, the store, the shop, upon the highway or in the silence of the woods they will not be alone."

Justice by Lynching

In April 1854, a lynch mob hanged two Snohomish Indians on a stump at 1st Avenue and Main Street. The mob felt that the Indians had murdered a Pennsylvania man and buried his body on the shore of Lake Union. Sailors retrieved a block and tackle from their ship at Yeslers wharf and the mob broke into the cabin where the two accused Indians were being held, dragged them to the street corner, and hanged them. A third Indian was held at a different location, tried, and found to be innocent.

In October 1881, Seattle Police Officer David Sires was in James Smith's Saloon on Washington Street near 2nd Avenue. He was not wearing his uniform when he heard a gunshot outside and went to investigate. Witnesses pointed out a man up the street who was running away. Sires gave chase and caught up with the man at 3rd Avenue and Mill Street (now known as Yesler Way). The man stopped in front of Madame Malla's, turned, and warned Sires to stay back, thinking that Sires was a thug. As Sires approached without identifying himself as a police officer, the man shot him in the throat and fled. Madam Malla heard the shot, found Sires in the street, and blew her police whistle to summon help. There were no witnesses to the shooting and no gun was found, so the responding officer, a man named Payne, said that the shooting was an accident, making Sires Seattle's first police officer killed in the line of duty. A fellow officer, Jim Woolery, traced Payne to a room at Aldus Restaurant and arrested him. Payne was held for trial in the city jail, but Seattle is an impatient town.

On January 18, 1882, a mob seized two other men accused of murder outside of court and lynched them in the trees on the north side of James Street between 1st and 2nd Avenues. At that point, someone shouted that the mob should go after Payne. The mob stormed the jail and other prisoners pointed him out. He protested his innocence, but was dragged out and hanged next to the other victims. Before dying, he cried out, "You hang me, and you will hang an innocent man."

The city of Seattle left the boards and the two maple trees used to lynch the suspects in place as a warning to future criminals until the next spring. No one was ever arrested for the lynching and the jury found that those lynched came to their death "...by hanging, but from the evidence furnished we are unable to find by whose hands. We are satisfied that in his death substantial and speedy justice has been served."

A City Destroyed

Seattle's Great Fire of 1889 leveled most of the city and the founders raised the city streets to provide drainage. These raised streets were eventually covered and enclosed and the lower chambers were eventually sealed off and forgotten; used only by vagrants, bootleggers, and women of low repute. At census time, the local prostitutes would identify themselves as seamstresses, so the city instituted a sewing machine tax!

Seattle's first hotel, the Felker House, was built on 1st Avenue and Main Street. Mary Ann Conklin, who later added a brothel to the top floor, ran it. Mary Ann reportedly died in 1873 and the wooden hotel later burned to the ground in the Great Fire of 1889. Her remains were originally buried in Seattle's first municipal cemetery. When that cemetery was made into Denny Park, the bodies were moved to Lakeview Cemetery in 1884. While moving Mary's coffin, it took six men to raise it. They removed the lid to find that her body had turned to stone, with all her features intact. She now lies beneath a simple stone that attests to her personality in life...

The Totem Pole

In October 1899, a sixty-foot totem pole from Fort Tongass in Alaska was unveiled in Seattle's Pioneer Square. This totem stands in front of Doc Maynard's Saloon.

"Mother Damnable Conklin Died 1887."

The gathered crowd cheered the totem pole that was presented to the City of Seattle by the Chamber of Commerce "Committee of Fifteen." Later reports indicated that this committee of citizens had stolen the totem from an Alaskan Indian Village!

The Seattle Post Intelligencer newspaper sponsored a good will committee of leading citizens on a tour of Alaska. When the ship, City of Seattle, stopped at Fort Tongas, according to third mate McGillvery:

"The Indians were all away fishing, except for one who stayed in his house and looked scared to death. We picked out the best looking totem pole... I took a couple of sailors ashore and we chopped it down—just like you'd chop down a tree. It was too big to roll down the beach, so we sawed it in two."

The Tlingit Tribe declared the totem stolen and demanded $20,000 for it, but settled for $500, which was paid by the newspaper. A federal grand jury in Alaska indicted eight of Seattle's citizens for theft of government property, but the suit was dismissed.

On October 22, 1938, an arsonist attempted to destroy the totem by starting a fire in the mouth of the image at the bottom of the totem. It was seriously damaged. The totem was removed and replaced in 1940 with a replica that was carved by the descendants of the carvers of the original totem. More recently a man

This central Totem marks the start of Doc Maynard's Underground Tour.

climbed to the top of the totem to stage a protest, but slipped off and fell to the concrete below. He was killed on impact.

~~~~~

The Court at Pioneer Square
401 2nd Avenue, Suite 100

People who work here share stories of noises in the dark evenings and of the resident ghost "Bob," who breathes down people's necks and bangs on pipes in this old building.

The Central Saloon
207 1st Avenue South

Built in 1892 as the Watson Brothers Famous Restaurant, in 1901 it changed owners and became known as The Seattle Bar. In 1919, it was named the Central Café and most recently as "The Central." This building has a rich history and was a café, a post office, an employment hall, a card hall, and a brothel. The dumbwaiter that served the brothel is still at the north wall of the building.

People have reported hearing things moving around in the upstairs offices when no one was about. One employee looked up and saw an older woman wearing a long skirt and white shirt as if it was the 1800s. Her hair

The Central Saloon was a café, a post office, a card hall, and a brothel!

was in a tight bun on the top of her head. When the observer looked away and then looked back, the female ghost had vanished. One worker heard the sounds of things banging around and doors opening and closing and assumed it was the cleaning people. She was informed later on that there was no cleaning staff. She reported seeing an older woman with a bun on the top of her head one night when she was leaving. The vision had a long skirt with a white shirt and disappeared when the worker looked away. The upper floors where the apparition has been seen was the old bordello that later became offices.

Doc Maynard's
608 1st Avenue

Located between Cherry and Yesler streets, Doc Maynard's is a restored 1890s pub that is reported to be haunted by a ghost that doesn't like music. It's also the starting location of the Seattle Underground Tour. During the tour, the ghost of another man dressed in formal attire and a bank guard have been seen. Paranormal activity has been reported near the base of one of the hotels that seems to be shimmering with spirits, according to a local ghost-hunting group.

Tourists gather at a Doc Maynard's to meet their guide, who will describe Pioneer Square's history of plumbing catastrophes, scandals, and misadventures. Then participants are guided into parts of the city fourteen feet below the current streets, climbing through old abandoned areas, exploring history, and learning about some of the more seedy parts of town and the ghostly activity that tends to happen there. This year-round tour takes about ninety minutes and costs $11, which must be paid in cash. The schedule varies, and is first come/first served. A motorized tour of eccentric Seattle runs Tuesdays through Saturdays in the summertime. This ninety-minute tour is for adults only since the $20 fare includes a cocktail afterwards. For more information, call 206-682-4646 or visit their website at www.undergroundtour.com.

Opposite page:
Doc Maynard's Saloon hosts underground
tours of haunted Seattle! Ask for Bryan!

Arctic Club Building
700 3rd Avenue

Around the corner and up the street from Doc Maynard's is the Arctic Club building located on Cherry Street. This building has sculptures of walrus' adorning its walls. The original artwork is still impressive, as is the "Dome Room" located on the third floor that is often used for parties and meetings.

The landmark building was built in 1917 by the Arctic Club, a private organization of entrepreneurs, industrialists, and artists with trade ties to Alaska. It was used by the City of Seattle for years and sold in 2005 to Arctic Club LLC. In the summer of 2008, it reopened with a luxurious 120-room hotel that combines the grandeur of the early men's club with first-class amenities for visitors to Seattle. Their website is www.arctichotelseattle.com. The foyer and stairwells are lined with Alaskan marble and twenty-seven molded walrus heads adorn the third floor exterior.

The Arctic Hotel... Marion Zioncheck threw himself out a window and landed in front of his wife, who was coming to join him for lunch!

The dome room of the Arctic Hotel is open for viewing and was used in Stephen King's movie, "Red Rose."

The Northern Lights Dome Room is one of the grandest event facilities in Seattle and was featured in the movie "Red Rose" as a library. The hotel management has maintained the architecture and artifacts that speak of the Alaska-Yukon Pacific Exposition when the Arctic Club was established by those adventurers who found their fortune in the 1908 gold rush. The hotel is truly first class, along with its lounge (The Polar Bar) and restaurant (Juno). Don't forget their valet parking. When was the last time a ghost hunter could valet park and then check out the local haunts? Try to stay on the fifth floor facing Third Street. Orbs have been seen there.

The building may have its own spirit spending time there: the honorable Congressman Marion Zioncheck who had an office on the fifth floor. Marion had moved from Poland to Seattle with his working-class parents. He attended the University of Washington and earned a law degree while making a name for himself as a left wing leader in the Democratic Party. He was elected to Congress at the age of thirty-two and was an ardent supporter of the working class and FDR's New Deal. His escapades included dancing in the fountains of Washington, DC and driving on the White House lawn. He was evicted from his Washington, DC apartment after a dispute with his landlord, was involved in a student riot, and was caught throwing coconuts from a hotel window. This colorful Congressman also judged a beauty contest in a nightclub, getting into a fight with one of the losing contestants boyfriends afterwards. On New Year's Day in 1936, he went to the switchboard of a major DC hotel and rang each and every room and wished them a happy New Year. This amusing prank was picked up by the newspapers.

Louise Nix, who worked for the WPA as a secretary, contacted Marion and asked him out. Within a week, he announced their engagement with his usual flair, wearing an Indian headdress and carrying a bow and arrow. He married her after their first date, and Marion became famous for his drunken escapades and extracurricular antics with his new wife, including a late-night frolic in a Washington, DC fountain. As these escapades continued, some people — especially those who disagreed with his politics and FDR's New Deal — began to consider that there might be some sanity issues with this new Congressman. He was sent to a mental institution, but escaped from the facility on Independence Day in 1936.

Marion was a two-term member of Congress and a good friend of King County Prosecutor Warren Magnuson. In 1936, when the press regaled him, he became depressed and mentioned to his friend Magnuson that he may not seek reelection. Warren Magnuson filed to run for the 1st District's congressional seat — Marion's seat — on August 1, which further depressed the young congressman. Five days after Magnuson filed the political papers, Zioncheck filled out his will and left a farewell note on his desk that read:

"My only hope in life was to improve the condition of an unfair economic system that held no promise to those that all the wealth of even a decent chance to survive let alone live."

He told his brother-in-law that he was going to get his hat and went back into his office. His brother-in-law watched in horror as Marion dove out the fifth floor window. On August 6, 1936, Marion fell to his death and his body struck the pavement of Third Street directly in front of a car that was occupied by none other than his young wife. Marion is buried in the Evergreen-Washelli Cemetery in Seattle. It is interesting to note that Bertha Landes, the first female mayor of Seattle in 1926, is also buried in Evergreen Cemetery.

King Street Station
503 South Jackson Street

This rail station opened May 10, 1906 and has a clock tower that is modeled after the tower at the Piazza de San Marco in Venice. The building hasn't changed much since the first photo was taken over eighty years ago as compared to the more recent photo (shown here) taken in 2007.

Invisible pedestrians still walk around the Safari platform. Legend has it that the Holy Roller leader Creffield was killed near the station. In the men's bathroom, clicking sounds can be heard as if someone was walking when no one was around.

The main hallway in the King's Street Station.

King Street Station has invisible patrons that walk the Seafair platform.

Check for invisible tenants in the men's room at the King Street Station.

Union Station
401 South Jackson Street

The station opened in 1911 and closed in 1971. After a restoration project, it reopened in 1999 and provides a gateway to Seattle's International District. Security workers report that lights turn off and on mysteriously, doors open and close of their own accord, and occasionally the sounds of children playing may be heard in the great hall.

Surveillance cameras have revealed shadowy figures. One ghost is supposedly a former railroad security officer who was killed by a train. Another is a woman dressed in a white Victorian dress. She has been seen several times at what was once the baggage level of the station, pacing in agitation. She normally disappears when she is approached. A security guard claims that the woman once communicated with her and explained that she haunts the station because she was raped and killed at that location. The bullet holes in one of the benches that line the great hall attest to the violent past of the station.

Union Station has its own spirits that close doors. Listen for children playing!

Capitol Hill

> ## A creative community that supports the arts... both living and dead.

Capitol Hill Methodist Church
128 16th Avenue East

The Rev. Daniel Bagley and his wife Susannah haunt the parsonage of this church. One report states that a resident saw Susannah surrounded by a bluish light in a flowing gown. The spirit asked the resident, "How do I get out?" The resident pointed to the door, but Susannah serenely floated out the upstairs window instead. The building has been listed as a historical structure since 1977 and is currently owned by a company called Catalyst.

Deluxe Grill
625 Broadway East

Located near the Museum of the Mysteries, at the corner of Broadway and Harvard Street, the Deluxe Grill was the first legal post-prohibition bar in Seattle. This popular grill has been the host of mysterious happenings, including pool table balls moving on their own accord and television sets that turn themselves off and on...much to the dismay of the employees.

Late at night workers often feel an eerie presence in the area. A waiter we talked to said he's seen full apparitions, as well as heard footsteps. In the poolroom, people are heard and seen walking around — even though they are not there.

Seattle Museum of the Mysteries
623 Broadway East

Located in the basement of a building between Mercer and Roy streets, at this museum visitors have smelled cologne or tobacco smoke in the area when no one is around. A ghostly man seems to enjoy playing with women's hair and a ghost-hunting group captured an EVP in the hallway. The proprietors of the museum may invite you to sit in at the poker table with them, or even spend the night in the museum!

If you are lucky enough to spend a "lock-in" at the museum, you'll experience a round of "ghost poker" in an attempt to prompt the spirit to show itself. Whiskey is poured for the ghost and EMF meters are placed near laying cards. The ghost is said to prefer to be called Alexander and is reported to be the spirit of a gambler named Peter Alexander Dunnovitch who used to play cards in this basement museum when it was a speakeasy during the times of Prohibition. The staff of the museum has had success raising the spirit by hosting a card game in his honor and riffling cards and clinking poker chips, which caused EMF detectors to signal that Alexander was nearby!

Kerry Hall, Cornish School of Art
710 East Roy Street

This school is listed on the National Register of Historic Places as a Performing Arts and Education site representative of the 1900-1924 era. Nellie Cornish founded the school in 1914 and had an apartment in the top of this building...and may still haunt this location.

Room 313 was part of her apartment, and people have reported hearing accordion music as if it was playing on an old record player coming from this empty room. Students say you are paranormally challenged if you don't have an experience. A student was carrying books down the stairs when she saw a finger sticking out of the banister; she screamed and dropped the books. Also a spectral woman in an old dress has been seen there.

Harvard Exit Theater
807 East Roy Street

This three-story red brick building, now a movie theater, used to be a meeting hall for the Women's Century Club, a women's organization of the 1920s. This club was home to Seattle's earlier feminist movement seeking equality for women.

Employees report seeing a woman sitting in the main lobby; she wears a long floral dress that seems to be from the early twentieth century and has her hair in a bun. Closer examination showed that the woman was translucent, and as one employee stared at the woman, she slowly vanished. This apparition has been seen often and is usually calmly reading a book. She may look up and smile in acknowledgment and has been known to turn off the lamp and walk out of the room. This may be the spirit of Bertha Landes, who was a member of the Century Club and also served as Seattle's first female mayor in 1926. When a museum in the Smith Tower hosted a display honoring Landes, her image was reported floating near the display.

Another spirit is seen standing in the first floor balcony wearing an old-fashioned Victorian dress, though her face and hands are not visible. People have also reported seeing the ghost of a woman hanging in the hallway, as well as hearing footsteps and laughter. The projectionists have found their film canisters rearranged in the projection room, and on one occasion, came to work to find the projector running and the room locked from the inside. Upon gaining entrance to the room, it was found to be totally empty.

Ghostly spirits have rearranged furniture during the night, as if the Women's Club was still having their meetings in the hall. A long time tradition of the Women's Club was to build a fire in the fireplace every night. One employee entered the theater in the morning after it was empty all night to discover a freshly built fire roaring in the hearth.

The second floor bathroom is the location where a woman reportedly hanged herself. People using that bathroom have heard a specter say, "This is a very nice bathroom." One man heard a woman crying in the hallway near the second floor administration office. He went to help her, thinking she was a live human being, but she vanished into thin air. Another time an Asian woman came running down the stairs in tears saying, "Don't go on the second floor." The employee had opened a door and saw a woman hanging there, crying. This type of report is common... that of a beautiful translucent woman wandering the lobby and stairwells, sometimes crying.

A lighthearted male spirit has also been spotted at the theater. He calls himself Pete. This portly man is dressed in old-fashioned clothes and

The Harvard Exit Theater is a favorite haunt of local ghost hunters.

probably pre-dates the Century club. Historians claim that in the house that was located there prior to the current building being constructed a man was murdered, and some say that the projector booth in the first floor often has sounds of two men fighting.

The third floor is host to an energy presence that does not have a personality, but a collective will of mass energy. Some refer to this energy as a "thought form," which may have been formed over the years as various groups met in the building. These meetings included women fighting for the right to vote, the Century Club women, and other activist organizations in the 1960s and 1970s. Theater renovations and séances may have stirred up this energy field, which includes a sense of oppression and hostility. Sightings of women in turn-of-the-century clothes occur on the third floor.

One manager investigated noises and voices heard on the third floor since no one should have been there. Though he didn't find anyone there, he heard an exit door closing. In hot pursuit, he attempted to open the door, only to find that it was held fast by a force on the other side. When the door finally opened, there was no one there. Photographers who have taken pictures of the lobby on the third floor have found images of people sitting in the empty chairs. Paula Nechak co-managed the theater in 1982; after she turned off the lights on the third floor, she reported feeling people behind her, watching her.

While spending a night in the theater, a group of investigators placed a magnet by the third floor exit door. They witnessed a large ball of energy move across the auditorium to the exit door, where it left the building, causing the magnet to revolve wildly. There may also be some type of primordial force that seems to attack only men on the third floor. Staff working alone in the building would hear doors rattling of their own volition; one employee heard the rattling doors and soon after left the employ of the theater.

As recently as October 2006, spirits were making their presence known. A local newsperson was on the third floor for a news feature. As the crew filmed the interview, the conversation turned to Ms. Landes and her contributions to the city. The reporter mentioned that although Martha passed away in Ann Arbor, her impact on the city of Seattle was widespread. With no wind, cars, or trucks in the area, the window next to the reporter began to rattle violently and loudly... apparently Ms. Landes was once again making her presence known.

D.A.R. Building
Roy and Harvard streets

Originally a church, this building has been owned by the Daughters of American Revolution for years. It is now rented out for social events. Witnesses say they have heard music and strange voices inside the structure and reports of a young female apparition dressed in 1800s vintage clothing, walking down the front stairs, have remained consistent over the years.

The Chapel
1600 Melrose Avenue

An upscale club in the Capitol Hill area, this bar is made of mausoleum stones and was built in the 1920s as a chapel inside Butterworth's Mortuary. Ghost sightings are a common occurrence.

Leaded glass window, ornate woodwork, vaulted ceilings, and enormous mirrors reflect the 1920s theme when the bar was the chapel for the adjoining Butterworth's Mortuary. Employees have reported that a glass flew straight up into the air and then smashed onto the dishwasher.

People report seeing someone in the balcony, and when they are sought out, the person is found to have vanished. One employee, who was accompanied by some co-workers, saw a woman in a dress appear in the balcony. She actually spoke in a surprised tone, saying, "I have...I have."

Other employees saw a fire burning downstairs through a grate in the floor, when there was no fire down below. The fire didn't exist, but was witnessed by numerous employees...in the exact same spot where the crematorium used to be!

And the flying glass? It's the exact same spot where the body of Bruce Lee was laid out!

Burnley School of Art
905 East Pine Street

Located at the corner of Broadway and Pine Street, this building was constructed in 1907 and has had many uses. It is sometimes referred to as The South Annex and once housed a high school gymnasium. There is a story that an eighteen-year-old male student at Burnley got into a fight at the gym after a basketball game and committed suicide or fell to his death on the school's steep rear stairway in 1913.

Since that time this student's spirit has haunted the building by moving objects and pushing them off shelves. Some folks have reported seeing his ghost while others have heard the sound of footsteps walking around. The strange occurrences include doors opening by themselves, loud footsteps of invisible beings, phones that are dialed by unseen fingers, coffee percolating without human assistance in older style coffee makers, and furniture being mysteriously stacked or rearranged overnight in the empty and locked school.

Students have reported objects hitting them, being pushed, or touched by unseen hands. A janitor once heard a loud crash in a darkened classroom. When he investigated the sound, he found that in the center row four desks and chairs had been overturned. Papers left in neat stacks have been found wadded up, desk drawers open and close, lights turn on and off, and doors open and close by themselves.

When a medium attempted to contact the spirit in the 1960s, a loud crash was reported in the upstairs bathroom. Investigators found a broken

The Burnley Building... where chairs stack themselves!

Jimmi Hendrix is commemo-rated on Broadway just down from the Burnley!

window and a huge rock that was too heavy to have been thrown from the alley below. Investigators using "automatic writing" said that the ghost led them to the school's basement and a hole into which the rock fit perfectly. Further excavation revealed a small animal's skeleton, but no other reasons for such a disturbance.

Séances were held using a stool in which the spirits could tap once for yes, twice for no. Instead of merely tapping once or twice, the stool banged and crashed around the room! During a 1968 séance, references were made regarding a left shoelace. At the conclusion of the séance, it was revealed that the left shoelace of every male attendee had broken that day.

This site now houses a dental office and the English Institute of Seattle Central Community College. An interesting side note is that a statue of Jimmi Hendrix is located one block north on Broadway and is worth taking a look at. Jimmi is buried at Greenwood Memorial Park in Renton, Washington.

Sorrento Hotel
900 Madison Street

Located at the corner of Madison and Terry streets, near the emergency room of the Virginia Mason Hospital, in the bar of the hotel's Hunt Club, footsteps may be heard and glasses move in full view of the guests. An apparition of a woman has also been sighted on the fourth floor near Room 408.

15th Avenue Video
400 15th Avenue East

Originally an old firehouse, this building still has the original "flip-open" fire truck doors in front. Four different employees have reported spooky forms and swinging staff doors. One employee saw an apparition of a man in old style clothing striding across the main room.

Mayflower Park Hotel
405 Olive Way

This 171-room luxury hotel was built in 1927. It opened under the name Bergonian and it has been reported that there are ghosts in Room 1120. In 1997, three separate guests reported a "spooky presence" in that room.

Marie Dempcy is the owner of the hotel and feels that the spirit is a friendly one. She believes that the ghost is the spirit of an older gentleman who had lived in a sixth floor apartment there for years. Employees have spotted the ghost going from empty room to empty room across the sixth floor hallway. One employee reported that the spirit moved his mop bucket to another floor.

The Sorrento Hotel has glasses that move themselves at the Hunt Club.

The spirit seems to be content with its surroundings and doesn't normally bother the staff, although renovations tend to increase the spotting of this friendly ghost...

The Baltic Room
1207 Pine Street

Both male and female ghosts have been seen at this popular club. Employees have reported activity in the upstairs linen closet, and a waitress reported an incident where a gray mist or fog passed between her and her friends.

During a renovation project, some of the large mirrors were removed from the walls using suction cups and an image of a woman's face was found etched into the corrugated cardboard behind the mirror. The woman resembled an evil vampire woman, complete with widows' peak wearing 1930s-style clothing and looking very harsh. The mirror was replaced.

A female spirit is seen dressed in a 1930s-style evening gown standing in the corner of the balcony overlooking the main room of the club and sometimes moves down to the main floor. Another spirit is a man in baggy pants wearing a fedora style hat with his dark suit.

The Egyptian Theater
805 East Pine Street

This little theater hosts the Seattle International Film Festival, seats about six hundred people, and is home to...a ghost. The spirit roams the aisles of the theater in roughly human shape and is usually spotted when the house lights come up and moviegoers are beginning to stir from their seats. However, this spirit doesn't seem to be attempting to get the attention of anyone.

Perhaps this ghost is one of the old Masons who performed rituals here when the theater was a Masonic temple, complete with capes and cloaks. Researchers report a dark and billowing figure that seems to be large and rotund, although there are no specific details. There have been no reports of anyone seeing the spirit's face, arms, hands, or legs. It is as if the ghost is wearing a hooded cloak that covers him to his ankles.

Elite Tavern
622 Broadway East

An apparition of a man has been seen upstairs and there are bullet holes in a stainless steel refrigerator. Perhaps Jimmy Buffet stopped by and got cabin fever?

22 Doors
405 15th Avenue East

At this club, ashtrays have been known to move by themselves and a wine carafe that was set on a table by a waitress shattered by itself, striking both the customer and waitress with pieces of glass.

Nathan Hale High School
10750 30th Avenue NE

Observers report odd noises and feelings of fear when walking through a certain spot in the hallways of this high school. Rumor has it that a student was raped in one of the halls years ago.

UNIVERSITY DISTRICT

Home of the University of Washington, spirits here refuse to graduate to the next life!

Serial killer Ted Bundy's former home is in the University District. We also cannot forget that Bundy started his killing spree in Seattle while he was a student at the University of Washington! His old residence can't seem to keep tenants. A dark feeling of foreboding seems to preside over this house where Mr. Bundy preyed on his victims and kept their body parts and heads inside a refrigerator.

It is rumored that the body of his first victim was dumped in the foundation of a building at the University of Puget Sound that was being built at the time. A body was never found, but a spectral girl has been spotted making strange noises and walking the halls of the University of Puget Sound in Tacoma, Washington. Check out the twelfth floor of McMahon Hall or the Elliott Avenue Apartment building, where it is said Ted lived. Spirits walk the hallways of the apartment building…and then disappear without any of the doors being opened.

University YMCA
5003 12th Avenue

Built in 1951, the YMCA is located at the crossroads of 50th and 12th avenues. After all the members have left the building and the cleaning crew is cleaning the basement workout room, footsteps and voices seem to come from the empty upstairs area. A presence has also been felt in the furnace room.

College Inn Pub
4006 University Way NE

At this pub, built in 1909 for the Alaska-Yukon Exposition, Howard is a local ghost that appears as an old codger in a khaki trench coat to knock back a few beers. This may be the spirit of Howard Bock, who arrived in Seattle about the time of the Yukon gold rush. People thought that he had been to Alaska and had a stash of gold hidden someplace. He was murdered in this rough and tumble town.

When the pub opened, spirits tossed things around on the shelves, tapped or thumped on walls, and turned on and off coffee pots. Reports have been made of a piano playing without anyone sitting at the keyboard and sightings of an Irish man in the back room.

Columns Amphitheater
University of Washington

This amphitheater is named for the four columns of the original University of Washington building that was located closer to the downtown area. A young male adult hangs around as a spirit, but seems to dislike visitors. The entity is said to prey on couples sitting on a bench by shaking the shrubbery violently and growling. Some visitors are uneasy entering the amphitheater at night...as brooding feelings of foreboding come over them.

Neptune Theater
1303 NE 45th Avenue

This theater at the corner of 45th Avenue and Brooklyn Street has unexplained cold spots and the smell of tobacco that have caused some people to name this haunting "The Smoking Ghost." Workers in the backstage area report the smell of burning tobacco when no one is smoking in that area, and a ghostly image of a woman has been reported in the lobby. A janitor once saw a woman wearing a long, dark-colored gown that did not walk on the floor...but floated five inches above it! Others reported a lady dressed in white with dark hair. One ghost seems to be a lady with dark hair in the organ loft (the Neptune housed the largest Kimball Orchestral Pipe Organ on the West Coast when it opened in 1921), swathed in white and surrounded by light. Another ghost hangs out in the men's restroom and the balcony; people who encounter the spirit get a feeling of immense fear. An employee was working late one night doing some painting and something pushed him from behind and nearly knocked him down.

Campion Residence Dormitory
Seattle University
914 East Jefferson Street, Seattle

Located near James Street and 12th Avenue, this dormitory seems to have an active spirit on the third or fourth floor, according to student residents. One student reported that at the beginning of the school year it sounded as if someone above her third-floor room was dragging something around, throwing things, and dropping bowling balls. When she and her roommate investigated, they discovered that the room above them was empty. Students report sounds of people running up and down the hallways, only to find that the halls are empty when they go to investigate. Showers on the third floor also turn on by themselves when no one is near by. Students speculate about the rumor that a girl committed suicide in the bathroom on the third floor.

GEORGETOWN

Settled prior to the Denny's arrival on Alki Beach, some say this is where Seattle began. It's also where the city's first airplane flight occurred...and the first fatal airplane crash!

These Georgetown locations are located directly beneath the flight path of Boeing Field. Seattle's first airplane flight took place at Meadows Race Track just south of Georgetown on the Duwamish River March 11, 1910 under the skillful control of Charles Hamilton. Legend has it that lumber magnate, William Boeing, observed the flight from the Duwamish River, where his yacht was being built. Apparently the founder of Boeing Airplane Company was not around when Mr. Hamilton crashed his rickety Curtis Reims Racer aircraft into a pond two days later. Two years later, in May of 1912, the same racetrack witnessed Seattle's first aviation death. J. Clifford Turpin was demonstrating his aeroplane when it crashed into the grandstands, killing one person and injuring twenty-one others.

In February 1943, one of Boeings top-secret XB-29 Super fortress bombers took off from Boeing field. This aircraft would eventually become the B-29, which would turn the tide in the Pacific and drop Atomic bombs on Japan in 1945. Twenty minutes after takeoff, this secret aircraft's engine caught fire and Pilot Eddie Allen turned to land the aircraft at the field. A second fire erupted and two crewmen bailed out as the aircraft narrowly missed skyscrapers in downtown Seattle. Their chutes did not deploy in time and they perished. The giant bomber slammed into the Frye meat packing plant just short of Boeing field, killing the nine remaining crewmen and as many as thirty workers in the plant.

In July 1949, a C-46 airliner from Air Transport Associates crashed in Georgetown, killing two passengers and five people on the ground. Seven Georgetown homes were destroyed and thirty-nine citizens were injured. The unscheduled flight carried twenty-eight military passengers when the left engine lost power on takeoff. Circling around the field to return to the airport, the plane cut through two power lines and headed into the residences on 961 Harney Street — five people in a wood frame rooming house were killed. The cause of the accident was determined to be that the wrong type of fuel was used.

In August 1951, another airplane tragedy struck as a Boeing B-50 bomber took off from the field, flying over Georgetown. While all of the engines were operating, the bomber seemed to lose power and turned toward the Ranier Brewery, where it struck the top of the building and cart-wheeled into the Lester Apartments on Beacon Hill, killing a total of eleven people.

Central Baptist Church
1201 Ellis Street

The Masons constructed this building in 1927. Not only is it the site of mysterious sounds and slamming doors, but there have also been sightings of a strange old man who haunts this Korean Baptist church. This was a former Masonic church and was supposedly used to sacrifice animals and possibly even humans in the early days.

Across the street from the stone marker that reveals the building's age is a psychic shop called Spirit Quest with interesting wares and services. Travelers may want to stop by and speak with owners Janice and Lewis.

Stellar Pizza, Ale and Cocktails
5513 Airport Way South

This club was a speakeasy during prohibition. It's been reported that the owner or manager died in a broom closet and perhaps it's his spirit that still haunts the place.

Georgetown Castle
6420 Carlton Street

A private residence that resembles a castle, this building is located across the street from Oxford Park and now houses Seattle's famous "Hat and Boots" structure. The hat and boots were part of a 1950s gas station and a visit there highlights the roadside attraction. The boots were the restroom for the Premium Tex Texaco gas station that opened in 1954. It was billed as the world's largest cowboy hat and boot display!

The Victorian looking house is officially listed as being built in 1902, but some people say that it was already standing when the Great Fire of 1899 destroyed most of the city of Seattle. The owner was reportedly found in the kitchen after committing suicide by ingesting carbolic acid—and some say she has never left.

Newspapers report that the home housed a social club called the Non Pariels; they either were a baseball team or sponsored one. In any event, the group built a stage on the first floor that folded up against the wall when it was not being used for theatrical productions. Later it was rumored that this same stage was used by exotic dancers who entertained at the house. Historians say that the top floor of the residence housed a brothel in the early 1900s. Then a nurse owned the house from 1937 to 1955, when she died.

Look for the big boots across the street from the Georgetown Castle!

A resident reported hearing a terrible fight in the room above his bedroom. A woman's voice would cry out, "No!" Then again, "No!" Followed by loud thumps that shook the ceiling as if furniture was being turned over and a body was flung against the wall. After a while, the activity dies down and the room becomes quiet. Then the sound of weeping and moaning was heard in the hallways…followed by frightened, helpless whimpers. When the resident went upstairs to check the upper corner bedroom, all was quiet— and empty. Not only was no one there, but there was also no furniture.

This scene was repeated a few nights later. Friends were staying over and, at 12:30 a.m., they heard a cry from the bedroom and the life and death struggle. The words "No! Manny, Manny! Oh, Manny…why?" were heard. Apparently in 1899, when the Georgetown mansion had been a brothel, a young Indian prostitute had been brutally stabbed to death and horribly mutilated in the upstairs corner bedroom by her lover, Manny.

Witnesses have also claimed to see a crazy old lady choking herself with one hand and hitting witnesses with the other. Her eyes have been said to 'burn like coal'. The lady is believed to be a Spanish woman who killed her

The Georgetown Castle has a female ghost with glowing red eyes!

illegitimate babies and buried them under the porch. It may be the spiritual survivor of a deadly lover's triangle in the former Georgetown bordello.

Another female ghost has been heard and seen on the property. This ghost may be Sarah, who was the granddaughter of the man who built the home. Sarah has been known to be helpful; in one instance rolling a loaf of bread across the table to a resident in the 1980s. The resident was hungry and was looking to make a sandwich, but was not familiar with the kitchen and where things were.

An artist who lived in the house kept seeing a female ghost and finally decided to paint a picture of the vision. He did a very nice job and hung the painting in the house. One day, a visitor came to the house and explained that she had visited her grandmother at the house years before. The artist let her inside to look around and when her eyes landed on the painting she asked where they had found the painting of her grandmother. The startled artist explained how the artwork had come to be and both felt comforted knowing that the presence was a friendly spirit.

Orient Express Restaurant & Lounge
2963 Fourth Avenue South

This train-themed restaurant was formerly known as Andy's Diner until 2008 and still calls the lounge area the Side Track Room. It is a restaurant built of railroad cars salvaged from the 1940s and arranged in such a way

The Orient Express is haunted by a beautiful female spirit that avoids workers.

as to form a wonderful dining area. Andy's served a fine dinner until it ceased operation and was sold. The new owners serve a dynamic Chinese/Thai fare in the same cars. The kitchen is still in the back and the rail cars remain in the same location. The car on the south side of the building is blue and was the personal car of Franklin D. Roosevelt and is marked as his inauguration car.

The ghosts here seem to be pranksters that rattle doorknobs and hurl silverware to the floor. One busboy saw a large headed black man limping down the hall into the cold storage area. He followed him, but found that no one was there. One waitress saw a shadow go around a corner of the restaurant. Visitors should seek out the head bartender, Byron. He has been at the property for years and is happy to share ghostly tales that persist even with the new owners.

People have also reported seeing a stunningly beautiful blonde woman about twenty to twenty-five years old; she vanishes when she moves to the rear cars of the restaurant. One witness watched this "hot babe" walk past the kitchen to the bar car, leading to the back of the restaurant. He followed her to the back where she vanished, even though all the doors were locked. Activity seems to be centered at the back of the restaurant, where staff will set up dining plates in a car and then return to find the tables had been cleared by an invisible hand and the forks, knives, and other silverware on the floor.

Jules Mae's Saloon
5919 Airport Way South

This saloon opened in the 1930s, was closed for five years, and then reopened in November 2004. Jules Mae is the name of the guy who first opened the bar. There's a gentleman ghost that lives in the back, near the pinball and arcade games.

METROPOLITAN SEATTLE

Across the city many ghosts have made their presence known...

The Aurora Bridge is the large bridge that carries drivers on Highway 99. Formally known as the George Washington Memorial Bridge, it was dedicated in February 1932 and spans Lake Union between the Fremont and Queen Anne neighborhoods. The bridge is 167 feet above water and is also known as Suicide Bridge: over 230 people have killed themselves by hurling themselves off the great height. The bridge has the second highest number of jumpers as any bridge in the nation. Only the

Golden Gate Bridge in San Francisco has more suicide jumpers. People have seen past suicides recreating their last dive on the bridge. It is said that a man jumped off the bridge with his dog to end both of their lives. People claim to still be able to see the chalk marks on the cement, and early in the mornings, about 2 to 4 a.m., you may see the image of a man and a dog on the cement staring blankly. Just last year (2009), the City approved a suicide prevention fence for the bridge.

In November 1998, the worst bus accident in Metropolitan Seattle's 25-year history took place as the driver (Mark McLaughlin) of a southbound bus was shot twice, for unknown reasons, by 43-year-old passenger Silas Cool with a 38-automatic as the bus was crossing Aurora Bridge. He then turned the pistol on himself. As the bus went out of control, it dropped fifty feet to land on the roof of an apartment building and tumble to the ground near the Fremont Troll, a large sculpture underneath the north end of the bridge. Killed in the crash were the driver, the shooter, and one passenger; thirty-two other passengers were injured.

Hamilton Middle School
1610 North 41st Street

This school houses a ghost in the second floor bathroom where the door opens and closes on its own. People in the bathroom report hearing mysterious footsteps when they are certain they are alone in the room. A rumor persists about a pregnant girl who died in the school.

The "Amazon.com" Building
1200 12th Avenue South, Ste. 1200

This building overlooks the city of Seattle from the intersection of I-5 and I-90. This was the old Merchant Marine Hospital that took care of many injured seamen throughout the years. Psychics can still sense a ghostly nurse who worked there. Some visitors have smelled the perfume that she wears as she strolls along the lower hallways.

Puget Sound Public Radio
4518 University Way (Suite 310)

Radio Station KUOW plays host to a ghost that haunts the station's studio and is sometimes captured on film as a dark figure roaming the halls. The spirit is said to be that of "Ole Johnny Mole," an actor who was known for his booming voice. This failed thespian is blamed for all types of mischievous incidents that occur at the station, such as rapping noises on microphones and strange signal noises.

Waldo Hospital
85th NE and NE 15th streets

The Waldo Sanitarium later became the Waldo Hospital. Attempts have been made to designate the two-story structure as an historical landmark. The building is currently leased to the Campfire organization and rumor has it that there are two underground streams running beneath it. Thornton Creek runs underground just east of Waldo. Running water may provide a portal or energy field that some feel make hauntings occur. Strange happenings have been reported in this building, including computers operating by themselves and books in locked rooms re-arranging themselves. Even the image of a female spirit have been reported by more than one person.

A former employee of Campfire heard the sound of footsteps up and down the hall and in a stairwell when no living person was visible. The elevator also tends to operate on its own; it has been inspected to see if there was a malfunction, but none was found.

The image of a ghostly nurse has been seen wandering around in the hospital as well.

Ghosts in the Parks

Glenacres Golf Course
1000 South 112th Street

In the 1960s, a gaunt, naked Indian was reportedly seen doing a twisting dance on the path to the golf course. Since then, hundreds of people, including police officers and news reporters, have seen a naked man on the trail leading onto the golf course here, performing Indian dances. When authorities attempted to catch the man, he simply disappeared. Regular appearances led to the idea that there may be an Indian burial ground beneath the golf course.

Green Lake Area
5701 East Green Lake Way

Numerous people have seen ghosts and apparitions in this area. At the swimming area, people have reported seeing swimmers waving their arms for help, as if they were drowning, between the dock and the beach. Another look reveals no living soul. Some venture that these ghost swimmers may be someone who died in the lake.

Gaines Point on the north end of Green Lake was named in memory of Sylvia Gaines, whose body was discovered on the north end of Green Lake June 17, 1926. Her body was dragged to the area near a walking path in a grove of cottonwoods. The body was arranged to look as if she had been assaulted, raped, and then murdered by being choked to death. Unfortunately, time has marched on and the city has forgotten about her, as no mention of Sylvia is left in this area.

Sylvia was born in Massachusetts in 1904. Her parents split up five years later when Wallace Bob Gaines moved to Washington. By 1925, Sylvia had graduated from Smith College and came to Seattle to get to know her father. Within ten months, this 22-year-old college graduate had been murdered. The case was riveting to the community eighty years ago. Her father reported his daughter missing and later identified her at the morgue. The prosecutor believed the father's story that a fiend had raped and killed Sylvia.

However, this theory began to unravel as investigators found that no neighbors or people walking by the lake had heard any commotion. This indicated that Sylvia was not killed by some stranger, but rather by someone she had no reason to fear. But whom had she been able to befriend in her short time in Seattle? Witnesses reported seeing Bob Gaines at the lakeshore around 9 p.m. that evening, near where the body was found. He had been seen bending down over something at the time. Other witnesses claimed to have seen Gaines drive around the lake several times at the time of the murder. Could the father have been the murderer?

After further investigation, the county prosecutor, Ewing Colvin, began to lay out the case against the prime suspect — a World War I Veteran... Sylvia's father! A father and the brother of William Gaines, who was the chairman of the King County Board of Commissioners, Bob Gaines was charged with the murder of his own daughter. Newspapers had a field day and wasted no time pointing out that Ewing was a good friend of the accused's brother, as the prosecutor investigated the death of the attractive 22-year-old woman.

A jury of nine men and three women was chosen. In 1920, women had received the right to vote, but many states still did not allow them to sit on a jury until as late as 1940. The media attention was so intense that the judge ordered the jury to be sequestered in a Seattle hotel to hear the sordid details that led to Sylvia's demise. She had been strangled and her head battered with a blunt instrument. Police found a bloody rock near the murder site. Testimony established that she had been murdered in one spot and then her body was dragged several yards away and arranged in a way that would suggest a sexual assault.

The prosecutor discovered the motive for the murder. It appeared that Bob Gaines had an unnatural relationship with his newfound daughter for most of Sylvia's visit. They had not seen each other since she was five-years-old and she moved in with him and his second wife, living in a small one-bedroom house at 108 North 51st Street. At first Sylvia slept on the couch in the living room. The trio argued frequently, as Mrs. Gaines became distraught over the situation, even attempting suicide in 1925 when Sylvia and her father threatened to leave the home and get their own apartment. A neighbor believed that Sylvia and Gaines were sharing a bed and that Mrs. Gaines had been sleeping on the couch. A Seattle patrolman reported that he had discovered Gaines and his daughter late at night in Woodland Park, not half a mile from the house and half way between the house and Green Lake. The couple had been parked in Gaines car as teenaged lovers might have been. An employee of a downtown Seattle hotel also testified that she had seen Gaines and his daughter in their nightclothes together in bed in November 1925. Witnesses described angry quarrels that erupted between Gaines and Sylvia in public. The prosecutor felt that Sylvia wanted to leave the house and stay with her uncle and that Bob Gaines had killed her to keep her from leaving him or revealing their incestuous affair.

Gaines testified that he had quarreled with Sylvia and she left the home at 108 North 51st Street shortly after 8 p.m. in an angry mood to walk around the lake. (The house still stands today.) He swore that he drove around the nearby streets looking for her and then drove to the home of his friend and drinking companion, Louis Stern, about 9:30 p.m. His alibi proved his undoing, as Louis Stern took the stand and reported that Gaines had told him, "You know what I have always told you, that if anyone in my house told me when I should come and go and when I should drink and how much, why I would kill em... Well, that's what happened."

Colvin's closing argument stressed that Gaines had been sexually involved with his daughter for some months and that she was fed up and wanted to leave. On June 16, they quarreled and Sylvia left the house to get away from her father. Gaines supposedly found her walking near Green Lake and killed her in an alcoholic, jealous rage. According to the prosecutor, he then tore her clothes and dragged her body near the path, arranging it in such a way as to suggest she had been raped. He continued to drink heavily and confessed the murder to Stern, his drinking buddy.

The jury took less than four hours to find Gaines guilty and sentence him to die. His unsuccessful appeal ended in his being hanged August 31, 1928 in Walla Walla, Washington. The community planted cottonwoods on the north end of Green Lake and called the area Gaines Point, to commemorate the death of 22-year-old Sylvia. The trees grew for seventy years and provided roosting places for bald eagles and other birds. In 1999, the Park Department replaced the trees with poplars, thereby removing the last physical reminder of the tragedy, which may account for the reports of a female ghost that has been seen haunting Green Lake.

Sylvia's spirit can be seen wandering around the north shore area that was named after her. This pale apparition reveals only part of her face as she hides behind the bushes and trees. She seems to be afraid to leave her hiding place, and while she is usually seen after sunset, her spirit has been seen in broad daylight. Some researches delving into the history feel that she was not killed by her father, but by some other criminal. The trial was explosive and had they not shared an incestuous relationship the circumstantial evidence may not have been sufficient to convict him. Some ghost hunters and psychics feel that Sylvia is still seeking to identify her killer, or simply wants to see justice served and her father cleared of the crime.

Martha Washington Institute
6612 57th Avenue South

This nine-acre park on Lake Washington is owned by the city and is open during daylight hours. The land itself has an interesting past.

After working the California Gold fields, Walter Graham came to Seattle and worked in the Yesler sawmill. His land included what is now Seward Park and he planted an orchard along the area. Trees included apple, plum, cherry, pear, and chestnut. He decided not to plant in Seward Park because of the poison oak, which haunts the park even today. It was during this time that Asa Mercer brought women to Seattle (as memorialized in the film "Seven Brides for Seven Brothers") by way of San Francisco. Walter married one of the "Mercer girls" from the first voyage and sold the land to Asa Mercer, who went south to obtain more women for the growing city of Seattle. This second trip forced Mercer into bankruptcy and a passenger loaned Mercer money for the trip in exchange for this farmland. Hence, John Wilson built his farm near the center of the park site and dug a well near a large willow tree in 1866. That tree was thirty inches in diameter in 1919 and may be the site of ghostly activity.

Everett Smith purchased the land in 1889 and built a youth camp on the site, working with the YMCA. There is a huge Madrona tree towards the water side of the park and Smith carved a hollow stairway for the children to play at the tree. It is said that the stairway is built into the base of the Madrona tree, which was seventy-two inches at the time. The tree is located in the center of a wooded area between the remains of the orchard and the lake.

In 1900, Major Cicero Newell, his wife Emma Cicero, and the Women's Century Club founded the Parental School for Boys and Girls in the Queen Anne area of Seattle to provide resident supervision for delinquent children. This reform school moved to Mercer Island in 1903, then back to Seattle in 1914, until finally moving to the Lake Washington property when they bought the land from Smith in 1920.

The State of Washington took over the school in 1957. Photographs taken of the facility in 1966 show a swimming dock, gymnasium, and dormitories, all of which are now gone. In 1972, the city of Seattle purchased the land to be used as a park. City sketches show the layout of the buildings including the willow tree where the original well was built, the school buildings, driveway, orchard, meadow, and Madrona tree.

Legend has it that sometime in the 1940s or 1950s a janitor at this institution murdered several patients or residents after going insane. Some say he also murdered some of the staff. He carried the bodies to a nearby dock and threw several into the water of Lake Washington before being subdued by police.

Psychics report bad spirits at the ruins of this institution, where girls were mistreated and babies were supposedly dropped into a well. A clinic, orphanage, and possibly a home for unwed mothers were located down the shoreline in Ranier Beach, closer to Renton. People claim to see a faint shadow of a boy next to a tree. In 2007, a ghost-hunting group captured a photograph of a person by the tree when no one else was in the park.

Some investigators claim that they have explored the foundations, dock, and small forest that remain. The foundation and dock are long gone, but a small wooded area and part of the original orchard are still there. During their exploration, one of the members was "grabbed by the ankles by an invisible force that left scratches around the sock area." They claimed to hear footsteps and the crying of a woman or child. While they reported that the locals don't go near the area and cursed them when they asked for directions, this was not the case in 2005. Sadly, most park users are not aware of its history.

In 2005, a retired fireman told a researcher that his team used to drain the fire hydrants in that area and that the girls would hang out of the windows and whistle at the firemen. He explained that the Luther Burbank School for Boys was located on Mercer Island and that the staff would often threaten to send the girls there. He said the girls and the staff were a little "rough around the edges."

Chapter Four:

WONDERFULLY WEIRD IN WASHINGTON STATE

Washington State was settled by independent young men and women who ventured west to seek their fortunes. First in the lumber industry, then as a stepping stone to the Gold Boom of Alaska, many of these pioneers struck it rich. Others found hard times, disappointment, and death. Some left a legacy while others left spirits behind...ones that are still, it seems, trying to tell their story.

ABERDEEN

The city was founded in 1880 when the only way to get to town was by boat. By 1898, the railroad had arrived and Aberdeen began to prosper and grow. It was made up of crib houses, honky-tonks, saloons, and gambling and dance halls. There were also boarding houses, hotels, and a few stores. The town soon earned the reputation as the toughest city west of Chicago. The population was made up of mill workers, prostitutes, wild women, pimps, crooked gamblers, crooked saloon keepers, thieves, and murderers. Needless to say, there was an obvious absence of organized law and order. It was said that anyone with money was not safe until their pockets were empty. A man laying on the sawdust streets was a common sight at night. Most often, these drunks were knocked out with a lead pipe and, when they woke up, their pockets were empty.

Dance hall girls would entice customers upstairs after a few drinks where a bouncer would kick the victim in the back of the leg. Hidden in the toe of their shoes was a needle use to inject a poison snake fluid. The victims would often be taken by Big Joe and dumped in the back room of a saloon a block away. The poor victim would wake up the next day, sore, with empty pockets and in some cases...no clothes!

Billy Gohl's spirit still haunts this restaurant in Aberdeen.

The images on the wall reflect Aberdeen's sordid past.

Billy's Bar and Grill
322 East Heron Street

Located at the corner of South G and Heron streets, this one hundred-year-old building was once the town's pharmacy and then served as the local Red Cross. Later on, the first floor of Billy's Bar and Grill housed a tavern, while the second floor contained a brothel. This former house of prostitution now houses a restaurant and lounge. The bar is named after Billy Ghol, who lived near the place during the turn-of-the-century when the town's main industry was logging, fishing, and sailing.

Baby faced Billy was the secretary of the local sailors' union. He would wait until the sailors cashed their paychecks and became drunk. Then he took them out in his boat down the harbor where they were dumped in the middle of the channel. Eventually, arson, robbery, shootings, and murder were traced back to Billy and he wound up in prison.

Some of the ladies and a very infamous ghost named Billy Ghol are said to haunt the place. Lights go on and off at night, cold spots are abundant, and fog forms on the plate glass mirror.

This pub was once a pharmacy.

The inside is still welcoming Billy Gohl and his spirit friends!

More than liquid spirits are kept at this pub.

Hubbs Muffler Shop
817 East Market Street

Down the street from Billy's is Hubbs Muffler Shop, where visitors can see a life-size statue of Kurt Cobain, the leader of the rock band, Nirvana. Kurt committed suicide in 1994, leaving behind a note that read: "It is better to burn out than to fade away."

A framed copy of the death certificate is in the mini-shrine to Cobain at this muffler shop with an image of the singer on the certificate. When investigators took pictures, one of the images was found to be upside down, showing a vastly different image of Cobain that was unsettling to the eye.

Hidden in a muffler shop is a tribute to former Nirvana band leader Kurt Cobain.

ARLINGTON

Arlington High School
18821 Crown Ridge Boulevard

At the old Arlington High School, a worker doing maintenance work fell from the roof of the auditorium. He broke his neck when he landed on the back of one of the chairs and his spirit has been reported walking at night on the top floor of the school and in the auditorium.

A cheerleader has also been seen stalking the halls, and there have been rumors of a hidden chamber or "lost room" underneath the high school that may be an old civil defense bomb shelter.

AUBURN

Cinema 17 Super Mall Theater
1101 Super Mall Way

With theatrical hauntings also listed in Bellingham, Kent, Seattle, and Tacoma, ghosts, in general, seem to enjoy theaters — and the Cinema 17 Super Mall Theater is no exception. A spirit has been reported hanging around the projection area of this theater, as projectors turn on and off by themselves in theaters 2, 9, and 17 for no apparent reason.

Fred Meyer Shoe Store
801 Auburn Way North

The Fred Meyer Shoe Store has a ghost that seems to have a dislike for shoes…yet it hangs around in the shoe department and the stockroom. Employees and customers have reported shoes being thrown at them and the sound of boxes being moved around when no one is there.

Auburn High School Auditorium
800 Northeast 4th Street

At this auditorium, a young girl has been sighted wandering around the pit area and in the catwalk. It has been reported that a girl fell from the catwalk during a production in the 1950s.

Neely Mansion
18008 59th Avenue Northeast,
Arlington, WA 98223-6353

An historical building from about 1894, the Neely Mansion Association is known to host tours for school children. The Victorian home is located off State Highway 18 at the foot of the Auburn/Black Diamond exit, east of Auburn.

During some of these tours, the children have wanted to know "who are the two kids playing upstairs" ... even though no children were visible upstairs. Visitors have seen the two children inside the mansion while others have seen the visage of a boy and a girl looking up at the windows from outside. Most of the activity seems to take place upstairs. Reports of toys moving by themselves have also been made.

BELLINGHAM

Old Town Café
316 West Holly Street

Located in the "Overland Block" area of Bellingham, the building was constructed in the 1890s. Passersby have reported hearing piano music... even though there is no piano inside the building.

A ghostly woman has been seen on the second floor when the building is empty. Employees also reported observing dishes floating for fifteen minutes and then returning to their original place after closing time.

Spectral beings often come to visit the Old Town Café.

Mount Baker Theatre
104 North Commercial Street

The theatre has a ghostly woman that seems to want nothing more than to watch over her property and its present owners. The building was constructed in 1927 and the story is that in order to build it they had to evict a woman named Judy from the building that previously stood there. This woman is reported to be the spirit that hangs around the theater and some people have taken pictures of her. After the show is over, when most of the customers have left, a rush of cold air is often felt and floating orbs or balls of light have been seen.

Don't be surprised to see a ghost in the aisle at the Mount Baker Theatre.

Mount Baker Theatre maintains its old charm.

Is it the lighthouse that attracts ghosts to the Mount Baker Theatre?

Shuksan Rehab Center
1530 James Street, Bellingham,
WA 98225

At Shuksan Rehab Center, objects move all by themselves in the rooms, call lights go on and off, and you can hear someone walking with a walker in the middle of night. Two registered nurses saw ghosts in the hallway that then walked through the door. The building was constructed on a lot where an old school existed from the 1800s into the 1950s.

Cemetery Hauntings

† Spirits or apparitions have been seen floating along the stone walls of Bayview Cemetery at 1420 Woburn Street. However, the spirit activity is not limited to the stone walls; there are at least two other hot spots: a monument called "The Deathbed" and another called "Angel Eyes." Locals say that if one lays on the deathbed...it will expedite death.

† In the Black Diamond Cemetery, one can see the swinging lights of a coal miner's lantern. People can also sometimes hear whistling in the wind, supposedly that of the coal miners. It is reported that a white horse has also sometimes been seen trotting around the headstones.

BREMERTON

Chester Manor Apartments
704 Chester Avenue

Designated as the Frank Chopp place in 2005, the apartment building is low-income housing near the downtown area. It was noted during the dedication ceremony that Frank was born in the building in 1953 when it was known as Harrison Hospital. In 1911, the hospital opened on this site as a four-story building and contained fifty-six rooms for patients and a morgue in the basement.

The building has gone through various phases and was once a haven for crime and drugs. Ghostly nurses, patients, and orderlies have been seen roaming the halls and rooms of this fifty-six-unit complex. Ghost hunters filming in the building found anti-ghost graffiti on a wall that they videotaped. The graffiti said: "**** you spirits..." Though the crew had heard nothing during the filming, when they reviewed the tape they heard a loud squeal and a thump. A still photo taken at that time revealed a white orb.

There are strange goings on at the Chopp House.

One newspaper delivery person saw the spirit of an old man with an IV bag walking down the halls. Another person reported seeing an old guy walk out of the elevator doors, which were closed at the time. A spirit of a red-haired woman wearing an old-fashion green dress has also been spotted in the halls.

In 1996, a resident reported hearing the voice of a child outside their door yelling, "Mommy, wait up," but when she looked out into the hallway there was no one there. Another woman reported seeing a faded green-colored ghost walking down from the third floor wearing a white nightgown. She didn't see the head of the ghost since the spirit was still coming down from the third floor! Another resident tells of a babysitter who put a child to bed and saw a man laying next to her daughter wearing a robe that only covered the top half of the body. There were no arms on the ghost...only bloody stumps. The vision vanished when the little girl screamed. People outside the building have reported seeing spirits watching them from inside empty rooms, as if they were interacting with the people on the sidewalk.

Bremerton Community Theatre
599 Lebo Boulevard

At this theater, the spirit of a man wearing a cape and top hat has been reported. Strange sounds can be heard and ghostly activity happens in the catwalks as well as in the girls' bathroom.

This modern theater is also haunted.

CARNATION

On Fall City/Carnation Back Road, there have been reports of a white ghostly looking dog. Witnesses say they would drive three miles down the road, where they find the dog sitting and watching them.

The Carnation Cemetery is located on Highway 203 next to the Carnation Elementary School. It was established as the Tolt Cemetery in 1905 and renamed the Carnation Cemetery in 1944. Witnesses report hearing footsteps and whispers and seeing figures out of the corner of their eyes, but it's the apparition of a woman in a white dress that has most often been reported... she is often seen in the company of a little boy.

CHENEY

Eastern Washington University
526 5th Street

The door of Room 203 in Dryden Hall may possess the spirit of a former student. It is said that a young man took his life inside during the 1960s and a contorted face may be seen in the wood grain of the door.

Residents of the second floor also report feelings of panic, odd odors, and cold spots.

CONCRETE

Mount Baker Hotel
45951 Main Street

Visitors to the hotel should prepare themselves for when they go upstairs. There, a little ghost girl about four-years-old with red hair and wearing blue jeans shorts and a pink shirt hangs out — and she has been reported to try to push visitors down the stairs. Fortunately, "she" doesn't succeed; guests have said that all they feel is a sort of tingling going through their body.

The little girl's voice can be heard saying, "The bad woman's gonna hurt me!" Visitors also report hearing, "Turn around — the bad woman will hurt you!" Rumor has it that her mother beat her to death.

The Mount Baker Hotel is a haunted reminder of Concrete's heyday.

DES MOINES

Des Moines Marina Park
22030 Cliff Avenue South

The birthplace of the city of Des Moines. The ghost of a little girl named Diana has been seen walking the beach and swinging on the swing set at the beach park at night every January 8th.

Children can be mischievous and their spirits seem to maintain this characteristic. Ghost hunters have felt themselves being pushed on the ridge overlooking the park, either by Diana or other little spirited children. One psychic researcher reported seeing a child with a broken arm that was attempting to lure her towards the spot on the cliff where the child had fallen and gotten hurt. According to the psychic, the child wanted to show investigators the slippery spot on the ridge trail overlooking the swing sets that he had fallen from. Orbs have been photographed near the swing sets, the barn picnic pavilion, and on the beach. Psychics have reported ghostly beings that seem to watch the ghost hunters with amusement and even disdain. Video cameras have been known to malfunction in certain areas.

In one instance, ghost hunters got a feeling of foreboding from a small building near the Puget Sound beach on the property. Psychics reported that the entity inside was gruff and didn't want the team there. A man, who was not with the group, had a video camera with him and reported that each time he tried to film inside the building through a slightly open door, his camera would shut off. He did this repeatedly, and AGHOST had their technician film the incident several times.

Other investigators reported that their cell phones would go off repeatedly during the expedition, even though they had turned them off as they always do during ghost hunts. Visitors have smelled a sweet perfume near the entrance to the beach, which lasts about a minute and then fades away. No one has been able to trace the source of the scent, which seems to accompany batteries in electronic devices being drained of power, even though they were fully charged a moment ago.

The park used to be an orphanage and the children played in the area. The orphanage had a maintenance man who lived on the property and it may be his spirit that remains, watching over the spirits of the children.

Bear in mind that this city park is closed from dusk to dawn; investigators who would like to explore this "anniversary ghost" after normal visiting hours must obtain permission from the Des Moines Parks and Recreation Department. They willingly provide access to the park after normal hours and notify the police department that an investigation is taking place.

EDMONDS

Frances Anderson Leisure & Cultural Arts Center
700 Main Street

Built in 1929, numerous spirits haunt the Frances Anderson Leisure and Cultural Arts Center. The original structure was called Edmonds Elementary School and is now owned and operated by the Edmonds Parks and Recreation Department. The center was named after Frances Anderson, a longtime teacher and principal for the school. Employees and visitors have reported haunting activity for years that involve spirits of children walking the hallways. It seems that the ghost of Frances Anderson herself, who died in the 1980s, can also be found hanging around her old haunt!

Edmonds Theater
415 Main Street

Located a few blocks away from the Arts Center, a male ghost can be found at Edmonds Theater. There seems to be the glowing and shadowy spirit of a man haunting this theater. Witnesses often report seeing this specter floating down the aisle with its glowing aura surrounding it.

ELLENSBURG

Ellensburg was competing to become the capital of the state in that late 1890s. It was also the site of some gruesome crimes committed by a man named Greg who lived in a building that once stood at 206 East Tacoma Street. It is said that Greg was the offspring of a satanic brother and sister who got married. Greg grew up under their influence and one day began kidnapping local children for use in ritual sacrifices. The townspeople formed a lynch mob, but before they got to Tacoma Street, Greg killed himself and set his house on fire. The flying embers ignited the rest of the buildings in Ellensburg, burning most of the city to the ground on July 4, 1898. With Ellensburg destroyed, Olympia became the state capital.

The story of "Inbred Greg" continues to be discussed in the 200 block of East Tacoma, which used to house the U-Haul dealership, Play and Pack, and Independent Auto shops. Today the building at 206 Tacoma between Main and Water streets is the home of McNutt Brothers Custom Electric. (Across the street at 205 Tacoma is the Papa Murphy Pizza shop.)

People have reported having encounters with a bearded Greg... complete with thick glasses, body odor, and stinky feet. The current manager of the U-Haul may share the spooky story with visitors; the old owner of the U-Haul had been known to hold séances and sometimes a sleepover on nights of a full moon.

Kamola Hall,
Central Washington University
400 East 8th Avenue

The ghost of a former student haunts Kamola Hall. After learning that her fiancé had been killed at war, she committed suicide on the top floor by hanging herself from the rafters. Over the years, people have reported strange noises and sightings. Resident students have complained of doors opening and closing when no one is there, as well as someone knocking on doors and then vanishing before the student can open the door.

ENUMCLAW

Hula Moon Salon
1525 Cole Street

The salon is located on the second floor of the Trommald Building. There was a fire in 1953 that destroyed the top floor and psychics report feeling the rush of people trying to get out of the building and difficulty breathing, as if there was smoke.

A female employee has reported seeing a man leaning against a wall when she was the only one inside. Shadowy images and fleeting glimpses of someone walking past the doorway have been reported when no one else was in the shop. This may be the spirit of "Jonathan," who seems to like the salon because it smells good and he can eavesdrop on the gossip. Vacuum cleaners turn on and off by themselves, lights flicker, and cupboards bang open and closed. The spirits also seem to enjoy unlocking the doors to the establishment when all the workers have gone home for the evening.

King County Fairgrounds

The old field house at the King County Fairgrounds was built in the 1930s and is now under the control of the city of Enumclaw. Employees have laughed about unexplained happenings there, including windows that are opened after staff has closed the building and secured it.

When the staff set up tape recorders to catch overnight sounds, they heard children's voices on the tapes when they played them back. County workers have reported hearing children's voices in the attic and basement of the building for years, although no children were around.

Staff at the hotel across the street have reported seeing the silhouette of a woman standing in the windows of the field house.

EVERETT

Everett Port is home to some haunted ships, including the 1880s-style schooner, the Equator, which is docked at Marine View Drive and 10th Avenue. Now an 81-foot floating museum, floating lights have been spotted on the deck. During a séance, it was reported that two ghosts haunt the ship.

The USS Fife is located at Perry Avenue and Fletcher Way. During its history, the Fife took the life of a captain, a contractor, and several crewmen. It is said that a sailor took his own life on the mid quarter deck and his spirit can be seen to this day. The engine room is the location where a civilian contractor died — he is still there. Engineers have heard sounds of footsteps, talking spirits, and, most bizarrely, duct tape being used when no one is around.

Everett High School
2416 Colby Avenue

It has been reported that a male ghost haunts Everett High School. When it was being built, a construction worker died. It seems that he was working in the auditorium and fell to his death. Many people have seen the man's spirit in the school and on the school grounds.

Everett Movie Theatre
2911 Colby Avenue

This old theatre is located in the downtown of North Everett. Several people have seen an apparition or ghost in the theater over the past two decades. The ghost is believed to be male: he may be an old theater customer or a former employee. Psychics have reported a supernatural presence in the theater.

Mariner High School
200 120th Street SW

Around midnight at Mariner High School, the lights are supposed to be on just as they are at any normal school. Yet, on some nights, the lights shut off by themselves. The story goes that if visitors are close enough, they can see "sensing" eyes staring at them from within the school. Only the eyes can be seen, which seem to be floating in space, sometimes with a soft glow about them. While the scene is too dark to see a body, people occasionally have reported seeing the figure of a man with wings.

Everett Inn
12619 4th Avenue West

The Everett Inn has been visited by a specter in blue or gray janitors' clothes, as well as some form of ectoplasm. Clanking sounds and a washing machine and dryer being slammed shut have been reported when nobody could be seen. People have also reported hearing a mumbling male voice in the basement near the elevator.

Mallard Cove Apartment
12402 Admiralty Way

This building houses the ghost of a taxi driver who, apparently, is still taking calls. Bill Stein passed away here in 1999 — and current residents report that an invisible person will pick up their phone, record an address, and then exit the apartment, leaving the door ajar. The ghost has been described as a forty-year-old man wearing a Mariners baseball cap and sweats, and is carrying a beer in his right hand.

FAIRHAVEN

According to legend, three Spanish war ships landed on the shores of what is now Fairhaven, a suburb of Bellingham that can be found at exit 250 off I-5. Spaniards began to construct a fort by creating a "mound" above high tide with a deep channel surrounding it. This mound was separated by water at all times and could only be approached by boat as the Spaniards began to build a fort called Ma-Mo-Sea. The Native Americans felt threatened and called on several neighboring tribes to join them in repulsing the invaders. In a midnight attack, the violent battle ended with many lives lost, but the ships were gone and not a living Spaniard remained...though some say that it is the souls of these early Spaniards that haunt the town.

In December, a "ghost train" is rumored to run through Fairhaven and Happy Valley as it makes its way down to the Skagit. The whistle blows, the wind blasts through, and the roar of the train is rumored to be heard. On December 21, 1892, a freight train pulled out of Fairhaven traveling southbound. Earlier, a train of logs had crossed the bridge across the Skagit, and the weight of it had broken the chord above the long wooden span and sprung the bent below. The watchman had discovered the break, and a carpenter's gang had been sent up from below Mt. Vernon to make repairs. The superintendent declared it safe for passage, much to the distress of the foreman. The bridge might be safe in two hours time, but the "super" insisted the train make the crossing. As it made its way across, the bridge broke and the train tumbled into the river, killing all three men onboard. Every anniversary of the crash, the ghost train runs. It runs over the same line, on a ghost track that hasn't been there for many years. It stops at stations that are but a memory, crashes, and clatters on to the Skagit at the wrecked bridge, and the locomotive drops to the bottom of the river, the end of the run...

The ghost train aside, the spirits of Fairhaven are quite active in town today. Almost every building lays claim to a ghost — Dos Padres has a very active one, as does the Doggie Diner building. Hangings regularly fall off the walls, and the staff often find open file drawer cabinets in the office upstairs. Apparently this was once the office space of the resident ghost — and she visits on occasion to work on her unfinished projects.

The Morgan Block, which currently houses Good Earth Pottery, served as a viewing area for the "Unclaimed Dead" as late as the 1900s.

When people died, they would be put on display here for people to claim.

Look for this marker in the cement to find the claims area for dead people!

During the 1890s and 1900s, thousands of transients came to help build the "New City of Fairhaven." Some died of exposure, some in accidents, and some committed suicide. When the bodies could not be identified, they were loaded into a wagon and put on display in hopes that someone could identify them.

Bellingham Bay Hotel
907 and 909 Harris Avenue

Built in 1901, the hotel originally housed a busy brothel in the Red Light district of Fairhaven. Decent women did not venture unescorted below 9th Street because of the bordellos and saloons. Current shop owners at Fairhaven Hardware, Nature's Window, and in the new Drummond Building have reported thumping sounds, store music going on and off, and footsteps in the halls.

Finnegan's Alley
1106 Harris Avenue

Just a few blocks away from the hotel is Finnegan's Alley. Owners of this Fairhaven pub site — both current and former — don't hesitate to talk about the resident ghost there.

First seen by a DJ, the ghost has been spotted many times as a blurred reflection in a glass door. The DJ stared at the image and watched it disappear.

The manager also reported receiving a gentle hug one day, and as recently as September 2002, she was talking with a plumber in the middle of the club when the TV came on all by itself. They stood around, a little shocked at the event, and talked about the ghost for a few moments. Then the TV turned itself off.

At Finnegan's Alley, DJ's have reported many ghost sightings in the building.

Finnegans Alley serves spirits of all types.

Nelson Block
Harris Avenue and 11th Street

Constructed in 1900, this corner building served as a bank for over thirty years. It is said that a seventeen-year-old girl died in a dentist chair there and continues to walk the halls.

In the 1970s, a human skeleton was found buried in the basement as the building was being renovated. Rumors persist of "someone" walking on crushed glass or sand at night in the upper levels, especially the second floor. Some people report seeing the partial apparition of a woman that walks through closed doors. Former restaurant employees in that space reported many disturbances, such as frigid air and strange noises after dark.

After a seventeen-year-old died in a dentist chair, people have heard her footsteps roaming the halls.

The Red Bus
Harris Avenue and 11th Street

Unknown footsteps and creaking doors are commonplace to the workers at Jacci's Fish & Chips inside the Red Bus, a 1948 English double-decker bus. Since their 1999 opening, employees have heard strange noises both upstairs and downstairs while working alone — and even Jacci was greeted one morning by a formerly broken stereo playing music.

Some speculate that the supernatural noises originate from the fifty-year-old bus itself, but knowing nothing of its British history, we can only speculate. However, the spot where the bus now stands was home to the Town Marshal's office in the 1890s. Marshal Parker left after one year in office for Buenos Aires with the city treasury. Perhaps he is now trapped here to pay his eternal penance.

Cranking doors and footsteps bother workers at this double decker bus.

The Quinby Building
1005-1007 Harris Avenue

The Doggie Diner

In the year 2000, employees of the Doggie Diner located in the Quinby Building were frightened by the sounds of drawers opening and closing in the empty office upstairs. When they investigated, an office chair rolled toward them as if pushed by an unseen hand. A computer typed things over and over. In the shop, shelves and pictures fell from walls and wall decorations flew nightly from one wall to the floor on the opposite side of the room. An employee was struck on the head by a clock that fell from the wall. The manager

reported that someone or something tugged on her ponytail and heard someone saying, "Good morning," though no one was around. Nearly all the staff has heard the sound of babies crying.

Always look beneath your feet for clues to haunted locations.

People have heard drawers opening and closing in the Quinby Building.

Off the Wall Antiques

A spooky feeling makes this shop a little cozier to ghost hunters. Sometimes people see a woman wearing a Victorian period dress gazing outward from the front door of the shop. The woman has an older hairstyle, and people in the store sometimes hear the sound of laughter through the opening that leads to the flower shop.

Witnesses have reported seeing a pack of crackers fly eight feet off a shelf! Another time witnesses saw chairs that were set up around a table in the front window move around as if ghosts were seating themselves! Keys and price tags have vanished, only to turn up someplace else, and books, glass figurines, and bottles have moved from the top shelves to the floor without human help.

~~~~~

Employees did not want to work after darkness fell at 1005 and 1007 Harris Avenue. When the owner finally sold the business, she was required to disclose the ghosts in the real estate listing. The current restaurant is Milagro's Mexico Grill and Katie's Cupcakes. Diners can wander around the place and investigate the upstairs dining room. This spot was formerly known as "Benton's Bath Parlor & Tonsorial Palace" and locals sometimes wonder if surgery is still taking place. There is a cement marker on the sidewalk outside the restaurant denoting the history of the place. Another cement marker is across the street that notes the place where bodies were put on display waiting for people to come and claim them.

FEDERAL WAY

In Federal Way, there is an apartment building in the 28600 block of 25th Place South. In April or May of 2008, spectral assaults may have taken place on two of the women who lived there. They claim that spirits have sexually assaulted them on weekend nights! They reported this to the management so often that the management turned it over to the Federal Way Police Department. The police department declined to give any information, but did mention that they had no solid leads in the case.

Ross Allison, president of the local ghost hunting organization AGHOST, took a stroll through the building, but remains skeptical. He says that sometimes strange things happen and people let their imaginations run away with them.

"And so they start to label every little interesting thing happening in their home as paranormal when it might just be a house creaking," he said. "A lot of times you'll find it might be medications that they're taking or something psychological."

Allison walked the area where the women claimed the spectral activity had taken place for two years, but the excursion was not complete. He could not locate any ghosts by himself. As a matter of fact, the two women reporting the events were also nowhere to be found!

FIFE

Emerald Queen Casino and Hotel
5700 Pacific Highway East

Ghost hunters often find records of an old Tuberculosis hospital near the Puyallup tribe that had its own crematorium. Naturally, stories of ghosts and haunted areas abound near such an institution as this, and people have reported seeing the ghosts of TB patients wandering around the hospital. When the hospital closed, the Puyallup tribe placed their administrative offices there, since it was said to be one of the sites of a village on the Puyallup River. Local people claim that the land is sacred and Native American burials took place there. Eventually the five-story building was razed to make room for the Emerald Queen Casino and Hotel (www.emeraldqueen.com/hotel.html).

This new facility is a very popular venue with rooms, banquet facilities, and entertainment. Ghost hunters who want to roam around the top floor seeking ghosts are welcomed, but be sure to stop at the front desk with identification and explain what you are going to do. Ghostly activity happens in the basement where the former crematorium used to be, but this area is off limits to the general public.

For best results, ghost hunters should spend the night on the fourth floor, which is purported to be haunted. The ghosts seem to hang around on the top floor of the hotel where children can be heard to sob although there are no living children present. A woman can also be heard crying and the sound of men moaning is heard as well, so researchers should bring their recorders to capture some EVPs. Also on the fourth floor, objects disappear from tables in guest rooms only to turn up on other tables, lights are turned off and on by invisible hands, and televisions are activated by the spirits. These same spirits will call the elevator to the fifth floor.

FORT LEWIS

This military base is located south of Tacoma and access to it can be difficult. Since it is a major military installation, it goes without saying that unauthorized visitors can expect to be detained. Still, the military police have been unable to stop the nightly sightings of ghost apparitions that are seen in the woods in North Fort Lewis. A few people say they have seen mysteriously cloaked spirits as well as the spirits of Native Americans.

Specific areas of interest include:

† North Fort Old Barracks
A former housekeeper reports doors slamming and cleaning carts moving on their own.

† North Fort Lewis
Cadences of platoons of soldiers running is often heard early in the morning...long before any unit of this size is conducting runs. Soldiers look outside to see who it is, and no one is there.

GIG HARBOR

Gig Harbor Grange
Wollochet and Artondale Drives

At the Gig Harbor Grange building, lights seem to go on and off by themselves.

Also, the recycle bins placed near the Grange were often disturbed during the night as if some former Grange officer was not happy with where the dumpsters were placed — they have since been removed.

Gig Harbor Grange has had a history of spooky events.

Index

Bush House Country Inn
300 5th Street

Built in 1889 for miners coming into the area, many people have claimed to see the apparition of "Alice" or "Annabel" at the inn. This young woman hanged herself at the turn-of-the-century when she heard that her lover was killed in a mining accident. As it turned out, her lover had not died, but returned home to find her dead. She hanged herself in Room 9 and Table 2 is her table...as her ghost still haunts the Bush House.

KENMORE

St. Edwards State Park
14445 Juanita Drive Northeast

Spectral children have been reported running around in the playground at this park, where Bastyr University is located. At Bastyr, there have been reports of cold spots and chandeliers that move on their own. In the basement, items around the chalkboards and chairs have also moved around.

KENT

East Hill Elementary School
9825 South 240th Street

A man hanged himself in a stairwell, and since then students and staff have seen the apparition of a man hanging there. They have also reported hearing him moaning and choking. Some children say that they can hear him whispering. Some people report that when they are walking near the stairs, they feel a chill and their throats constrict.

The Kent Station
4th Avenue and
Ramsay Way

Once an actual train station, Kent Station now houses an upscale shopping center. Visitors to the AMC Theater have reported ghostly happenings and some workers refuse to go into some of the theaters alone. Spectral activity seems to be centered in theaters 6, 7, and 8. In one case, a ghost hunter saw the apparition of a man move from the back of the theater to the front of the sparsely attended theater.

The Kent Station Theater has ghosts in its new AMC theater!

Bereiter House
855 East Smith Street

Home of the Kent Historical Museum, the Bereiter House is the site of strange things that have been happening for years. It was formerly the home of a local lumber magnate, Emil Bereiter, who built the home in 1907. It is located right next to the old Masonic Lodge on Smith Street.

In 2008, the home was being reconditioned and the lead-based paint was removed. Volunteers at the museum who work nights have reported experiencing odd feelings and uneasiness and hearing footsteps when no one is about and strange voices that cannot be accounted for. At one

The Bereiter House has ghostly footsteps and dolls that move on their own.

time a display of children's dolls was re-arranged by a spirited hand in the morning when workers returned to the locked museum.

A local ghost-hunting group has recorded a man's voice in the attic of the house, which workers have also heard from time to time. There is a set of stairs in the house that are steep — and both visitors and volunteers claim to have felt the sensation of being pushed down them.

KIRKLAND

The Williams/Web Building

Several residents have reported seeing a man in a hat and heard footsteps in the Williams/Web building, which is now a hotel and restaurant. Some people have seen objects move on their own, and workers in the restaurant have seen a shadowy figure. Others report seeing the spirit of a short man in a hat.

Central Tavern
124 Kirkland Avenue

A "pink lady" has been reported by employees and late night guests at the Central Tavern near the back of the room.

LEAVENWORTH

Edelweiss Hotel
843 Front Street

A charming Bavarian styled hotel located on the main street of Leavenworth, the Edelweiss has been remodeled several times in its one hundred-year-history. In the early 1910s, a fire devastated Leavenworth; in the aftermath, most buildings were made of brick. In the nineteenth century, this part of town was not the best part of Leavenworth and this hotel is rumored to have housed a bordello that was simply called "housing" since having a bordello would not have been appropriate.

There is also rumor of an underground tunnel that may have led between buildings that is now walled up. The basement is unfinished and shadows have been seen moving near the old oil tank. In the basement, fluorescent lights go off and on by themselves, accompanied by a clicking sound. Ghost hunters have felt themselves being touched on the head during investigations.

In the upstairs office of the Goldsmith store, a shop that sells gold jewelry adjacent to the restaurant, a previous owner had a heart attack and died. The

Never called a bordello, this "housing" building was witness to a brutal murder!

waitresses there wear traditional German dresses. It's been reported that one of the waitresses was sitting at a table on the main floor of the hotel years ago (when that floor was a restaurant) and was killed when a man shot her from the street. Rumor has it that the man was her boyfriend or husband.

People have reported being followed by spirits that seem to be making an effort to gain some of their attention. Some people feel that the spirits are not malicious and that they enjoy having them around. Cold spots have been detected and orbs have been captured in photographs.

Tumwater Bar and Restaurant
219 9th Street

There is a piano in this bar that seems to have a resident ghost attached to it. This spirit has been known to make pictures move on the walls, and investigators have picked up EMF fluctuations that could not be explained.

Long Beach

Lamplighter Restaurant
39th and L streets

Located in Seaview, the restaurant has a ghost that inhabits the bar. The spirit seems to enjoy playing pool while customers are playing the game. Patrons have seen the balls move by themselves and click against each other. The spirit seems to be a bit obnoxious and has been known to turn lights on and off.

Louis was the previous owner; he sold the restaurant in 1963 and is now deceased. When this eighty-year-old man died in 1977, poltergeist activity began at the restaurant. Louis' ashes were officially placed on the mantle in 1992 — and the strange occurrences seem to have stopped. Was Louis behind the activity? It appears so.

LONGVIEW

Monticello Middle School
1225 28th Avenue

At this Middle School, there is a legend that a young girl who had taken cookies to the workers died on the site while this school was being built. She was victim to a terrible fate when she fell in an area of freshly poured cement. Her ghost has been seen wandering the halls of the school at night, humming a tune. The girl's footsteps have been heard as well.

Heron Point

An old Indian burial ground, some people have reported seeing Indians walking the streets at night on Heron Point. There are other ghosts as well, including a tall man dressed black with a black hood that has been seen in the back of the park. He seems to enjoy frightening people by sneaking up behind them and whispering — and then disappearing when they turn around.

MARYSVILLE

Haunted Roadways

† Marysville-Pilchuck Road is located on the Tulalip Indian Reservation near Marysville, this road begins with an uphill drive and runs for several miles until it finally ends at an appropriate dead end. Motorists have seen someone running next to their vehicles, keeping pace, while looking in their windows as they drive thirty-five to forty-mph up the steep hill.

Indians have also been seen standing on the side of the road, but when drivers look in the rearview mirror after they have passed...the spectral Native American has vanished and is nowhere to be seen.

Some say they have even reported seeing people sitting in their backseat in the rearview mirror. When they turn to confront the ghostly hitchhikers, they find that they are alone in the car.

~~~~~

† On State Street, a dog by the name of Bud got sick one day and his owner got a gun and put him out of his misery. They say if you say his name late at night, a little girl appears and says, "Don't hurt him, he is my dog… Go away." She then stares at you and walks away.

Mission Park is also located on State Street. Three invisible children seem to enjoy playing the on the playground equipment there, which seems to move by themselves.

MONROE

The Chopping Block Tavern
116 Main Street

Located in the old part of town, this tavern has numerous sightings of spirits from bygone days when the town was a bit rougher around the edges. Customers have seen the spirits as well.

Tales of pictures and wall hangings falling down of their own accord have been attributed to a ghost as well as to the owner of the bar, who is reputed to be a Gypsy.

At the Chopping Block in Monroe, pictures fly off the walls.

Jeno's Restaurant and Lounge
123 Main Street

Ghost hunters have investigated this restaurant/lounge, which is located across the street on the same block as the Chopping Block. There seems to be a male spirit that walks from patron to patron in the bar, as restaurant regulars have reported his presence for a number of years.

Jeno's has a resident ghost that walks from guest to guest!

MOSES LAKE

The White Homestead

The White Homestead is a house that was built in 1903 and, according to actual witnesses, a murder took place there. Today, the ghost of the young lady with child that was murdered is still in residence. They have since moved the house off of its foundation and down the block, with renovation underway. The workers who have been there still hear the faint screaming of a young woman.

Haunted Schools

† Columbia Basin Alternative High School was located at 920 West Ivy Street. It was torn down in 2005 and the workers who demolished the building reported strange events during the de-construction. This haunting has been described as mysterious noises that happen around 11:30 p.m. An alarm has also been heard. A smoke-like apparition with only the legs showing is seen running down the hallway.

~~~

† On February 6, 1996, the way of life in Frontier Middle School was shattered forever when a student by the name of Barry Loukaitis stepped into his Algebra class with a high-powered hunting rifle and opened fire on the students. Since that time, both students and teachers claim they can still hear the echo of gunshots and the screams of the students from that part of the building. Many students attest to experiencing feelings of panic whenever they are in or around that area.

~~~

† In the theater at Moses Lake High School, the curtains will sway and lights will turn on when no one is there. A catwalk above the seats can be heard swaying even though the door to the stairway is locked tight...the stairs also creak even though the door is locked tight. People claim that in the costume room they can feel the atmospheric imprint of the spirits.

MUKILTEO

Harbor Point Middle School
5000 Harbor Point Boulevard

At this Middle School, there are three ghostly children that can be seen: one in the building and two little girls outside.

† The spirit boy has been spotted looking out a window facing Harbor Point Boulevard. He is rumored to be the ghost of Pete Anderson, a boy who fell out the window to his death. Some say a science teacher who didn't like the boy pushed him.

~~~

† The two girls may be the spirits of two sisters who were shot as they went to the school to pick up their brother. The two girls are visible, but fade away quickly if anyone stares at them for too long.

OCEAN SHORES

Shiloh Restaurant and Lounge
707 Ocean Shores Boulevard

Not only has a female spirit been spotted at this restaurant, there have also been reports of the lights in the parking lot going out and the cash registers malfunctioning for no apparent reason.

OLALLA

Salvation Heights is located on private property and is not open to the public. In the 1900s, Dr. Linda Burfield Hazzard ran a sanitarium in here. She felt that any disease could be cured by a method of fasting. It is said that she intentionally starved her patients to death and buried them on the grounds, planting a tree over each body. When she ran out of room for the bodies, she threw them off the cliff on the backside of where the building once stood. In fact, she had wills drawn up that gave her full possession of her deceased patients' money and valuables, which may account for some of the deaths. The foundation of the sanitarium and the incinerator in which she may have cremated some of the bodies remain today. The trees serve as headstones to the many nameless victims of Dr. Hazzard and remain a monument to "Starvation Heights."

OLYMPIA

Evergreen Ballroom
9121 Pacific Avenue

Built in 1917, this vaulted roof building hosted public dances, jazz, and alcohol during the 1900s when such activity was frowned upon. The building was designed to provide excellent acoustical sound for the dancers and the roof was added in 1932 to enhance the music.

During this remodeling, there was a manager's office and an apartment for the manager. One of the managers was Mary, who lived in the apartment and managed the ballroom in the 1930s. Some people who have seen this ghostly manager call her Aunt Mary. She seems to be observed hanging around near her old office. At times when the band played a slow tune she would be seen dancing by herself. This is the spot where the song "Louis Louie" was first performed. It is actually in Lacey, and the building was destroyed by fire in 2000.

Today there is just an empty lot and signs of housing that will eventually be built over the area. One wonders if those houses will see Mary's spirit from time to time.

McCleary Mansion
111 West 21st Avenue SW

Finished in 1934 in the style of English Renaissance, complete with billiard room and stained glass windows, this sprawling home now houses the Building and Industry Association of Washington (BIAW). Prior to the BIAW taking up the residence, though, the mansion had been converted into apartments and then housed businesses and government offices for the state.

One state worker stepped out of her office in 1992 and returned a short while later to find a young lady in her 30's sitting on her desk. The spectral image was in black and white, dressed in jeans, penny loafers, and

The McCleary Mansion has ghostly women from the 1930s that still show up to work!

a sweater. The spirit turned with a look of embarrassment and mirth. When the employee asked the woman to leave, she vanished from atop the desk.

In this ground floor office, which housed the Office of Archeology, was once a psychiatrist's office, where a woman had committed suicide a few years prior to this incident. Some people report seeing a vanishing black and white spirit in this area.

Janitors have heard the laughter of a woman in the empty building, and toilet paper seems to unroll itself in the ladies' room. At other times, books move off the shelves on their own.

However, instead of the psychiatric patient, some people feel that the spirit may be Ada McCleary, who was offended that her grand mansion had been converted to apartments and business offices. The BIAW has since restored the building to its original look.

OYSTERVILLE

This Northwest town was founded in the 1850s as a source of fresh oysters for California's hungry gold miners when Chinook Indian Chief Nahcati told the settlers about all the oysters in the area. The Chief lies in state at the Oysterville Cemetery and his grave is visited on a regular basis.

This National Historic Town is located at the north end of the Long Beach Peninsula. Visitors can stroll along the streets and view the church, post office, and schoolhouse retaining the historical look of Pacific County in the 1850s.

Oysterville served as the County Seat for the third county in the Washington Territory from 1855 to 1893. In 1875, residents built a County Courthouse and jail across the street from the schoolhouse. In the 1890s, the county decided to relocate the County Seat to South Bend, but the residents of Oysterville refused to yield the county records. During a quiet morning on Sunday, February 5, 1893, the "South Bend Raiders" stole the records and took them to their present location in South Bend.

Children could earn twenty-five cents for each bushel of oysters that they harvested and were selling to the oyster schooners at a time when schoolteachers were trying to keep the children from playing hooky. The current Oysterville Schoolhouse was built in 1907 after the town's older two-story schoolhouse burned to the ground. People say that a former student haunts the current schoolhouse. The child apparently died from an epileptic seizure and has chosen to remain in the familiar surroundings of the schoolhouse.

One student in the 1940s noted that the windows of the schoolhouse were high, but one day a feather appeared outside the window. It moved back and forth and caused a great consternation among the children. The feather would move along and then disappear…only to reappear on the other side. When the teacher went to investigate, there was no one there.

Ghost hunters can rent the schoolhouse for $50 per day by contacting the Oysterville Community Club at 360-665-2336.

PARADISE VALLEY

Paradise Valley Cemetery

Also known as Maltby Cemetery, this cemetery is hidden off the side of Redmond and Duvall roads. The map location is: T26N R6E Section 5. It contains about fifteen gravesites. Strange, unexplained things have been said to happen here, as people have reported seeing women and children, dressed in old, raggedy looking clothes, wandering around the gravesites.

PORT GAMBLE

Port Gamble is a ghost town that can be found overlooking the Hood Canal Bridge. The town was founded in 1853 as the perfect location for a sawmill. Named after Robert Gamble, a naval officer who was wounded in the War of 1812, by 1879 the port had been established as the largest sawmill town in Kitsap County. The town is also an historic village that hosts a ghost walk every October.

The Evergreen Paranormal Group claims that this may be one of the most haunted towns in Washington State. The group, AGHOST, has investigated the town as well and was successful in capturing numerous photos and EVPs. One EVP was recorded after a guide spoke, saying, "That's a lie! Liar! Liar!"

Like Port Hadlock (see next section), the village has its own ghostly spirit, which they honor in the form of a bottle of wine that is sold; it's named the...Port Gamble Ghost.

The hauntings

† An EVP was captured just down the hill from the graveyard in a brown guesthouse. Two ghostly voices, one male and one female, were recorded. The male voice says, "Hi, I'm Cecil. Please sign in here." It's followed by a female voice saying, "Thank you. I will."

And James Thompson is said to still haunt the upstairs of his old house in town, as three different visitors reported waking up in one of the guesthouses and feeling that something was sitting at the edge of their beds.

~~~

† AGHOST says the Walker Ames House, especially its basement, is very active. There is also a spectral woman that watches people from the third floor window.

~~~

† Lights flicker where there is no light bulb and spirit mumblings and children are heard laughing and running from the upstairs of the Post Office. During a walk-through investigation, an investigator said to a photographer, who was using a flash camera, "What are you trying to do, blind me?" On an EVP recording, a ghostly voice can be heard saying, "…tried to blind me, too. Get 'er…"

~~~

† In the Tea Room, a kindly ghost has an ear for music. A CD player will come to life and skip through several songs until settling on a version of Pachelbels Cannon in D Major. The lights would flicker in the main dining room and some have caught the image of a woman dressed in eighteenth century clothing watching the living.

~~~

† EVPs caught the voice of a male ghost underneath the General Store. Most of the EVPs are short, containing one or two words only. The store also has unexplained activity where cabinet files open by themselves and workers report hearing sounds of people following them. A spectral woman with two children has also been seen watching the living from time to time.

Port Hadlock

The Inn at Port Hadlock

Now an upscale hotel and marina, visitors arrive by car, boat, even floatplane to stay at this classy hotel with a fantastic restaurant. The hotel also has an art museum and the grounds are decorated with artwork that makes it a popular place for weddings and graduation parties.

The Inn is also popular with spirits. Linda Varner has worked at the hotel for thirteen years and Charlie, a maintenance worker, has been there for quite some time as well. Both of these people will share their ghost tales with you.

Before It Was an Inn

In 1911, the building was owned by Classen Chemical Company and was in full production, making ethyl alcohol out of sawdust. This historical landmark made alcohol until 1913 and closed in 1917. In 1978, Ray Hansen bought the plant and set about the task of turning it into a hotel and resort. He hired a maintenance man to work on the property during the transition. The name of the maintenance man was Oscar Sendbeck. When kids would sneak onto the property, the maintenance man would threaten them that if they didn't leave "Oscar the ghost" would get them. But there was no record of anyone called "Oscar" passing away at that site.

The Inn at Port Hadlock seems to be haunted by a spirit that the employees have named "Oscar." The employees had heard of an Oscar at the plant — and they all knew the story of the Classen Chemical Company's only accident:

The old chemical plant at Port Hadlock is now a haunted hotel.

Port Hadlock has so many ghost stories they named the house wine for them!

Legend has it that a new man started working at the plant and was known as "Shorty." On his first day at the factory, he had an accident in the where all the steam from the boilers collected into a small well to cool. When the steam cooled enough, it would become water again and drop into the well. One fateful day the cover was off the hot well and "Shorty" fell into the steam condenser. Workers responded to his screams and pulled him out of the well as his skin was falling off the young man's bones. With no drugs to soothe his pain, they had to carry him two miles through the brush and forests to the nearest hospital. All the way "Shorty" screamed and yelled as his skin hung off his body from the hot water dip. Once at the hospital, he was drugged to ease the pain until he died the next day.

The Spirits

Some feel that Oscar and Shorty are the same entity and they feel so comfortable around Oscar that Nemo's Restaurant has dedicated a wine to the spirit that is available to guests. It is called "Oscar's Cabernet" and the back label mentions the ghost that haunts the old plant.

This ghostly trickster loves playing with the late night employees between the hours of midnight and 5 a.m. near the lobby. Items will move when staff has set them down and then be found in a different location and lights swing by themselves when there is no stirring of the air, but most of the activity seems to occur in the kitchen area.

The kitchen had a bell that was used to let staff know that their order was ready. Late at night, the employees manning the front desk would hear the tingling of the bell as if some unearthly finger was pressing the button over and over in the darkened kitchen. The cooks have seen cabbage flip over by itself in the preparation area, and some people hear pounding as if someone was pounding on a pot. Doors also slam shut and lights go on when workers are trying to close up for the evening. In the lounge one night, all the glassware fell on the floor as if swept off the counter, yet nothing was broken.

The spirit also seems to enjoy turning on the karaoke machine in the lounge in the dead of night. One housekeeper, Linda Varner, decided to appease Oscar by "dancing with him" when this happened, and that usually resulted in lights and equipment being left alone.

Maintenance employees have found their decorations rearranged after they've all gone home for the evening. This has happened several times...it's as if the spirits are taking an interest in the place. Construction workers once heard a woman screaming from an empty break room. Her blood-curdling scream was accompanied by footsteps as if she was running across the hotel building from rooms in the 100's to the 200's, where no one has access to the unfinished floor.

Late one night the General Manager and a desk manager were working at the front desk when the heavy cash register behind them began to rattle and shake by itself until it shook itself off the counter. At other times, voices have been heard, taunting a female worker by whispering in her ear "I'm over here," followed a few seconds later by whispers in her other ear saying, "I'm over here." In one instance, a guest entered the hotel and immediately sensed the ghostly presence. He asked the management if there was something at the hotel, explaining that he had felt a presence as soon as he walked in the front door.

Images of a thin white female pass quickly by the corner when staff is in the office. The apparition vanishes out the back door. On the second floor, the spirit of a dark haired lady swishes around and moves things as she is looking for her child.

At other times the spirits touch the staff or play with their hair with cold or, at times, hot hands. Some staff members feel as if the spirits are trying to gain their attention with moans of extreme sadness that quickly change to excitement and pain. Perhaps the spirits simply want to be acknowledged and the staff has learned that if they write the events on paper as they occur...the record seems to satisfy the ghosts and calm things down for the night.

Some guests and staff have seen a man wearing a flannel shirt, dark jeans, and a big silver belt buckle. One time, when the spirit vanished in the blink of an eye, the witness heard a voice that said, "I think she saw me."

Haunted Rooms

The rooms are built into the old chemical vats, including the one into which Shorty fell. Current guests often don't realize as they gaze into the mirrored ceiling that they are, in fact, at the bottom of an old chemical vat!

There has been some interesting activity near Room 206 as well. One guest stopped by the front desk to ask if it was standard for housekeeping to shine his shoes, as his had been shined. No living employee of the hotel had shined his shoes in Room 206. The guest later reported odd things happening in the room. He also felt that someone was laying in bed with him; he could see the imprint on the bed, but could not see anyone in the room with him.

A staff member was checking the rooms and knocked on Room 206, only to hear a man's voice say that he would be just a minute. The housekeeper called the front desk and was informed that no one was checked into Room 206. Minutes later they approached the room, knocked, and entered. The room was empty and untouched.

Another guest refuses to stay in Room 212 claiming that they can hear Oscar shuffling around the room and making noises.

The following excerpts are from the night auditor's log book kept at the front desk. They detail the times and dates of the paranormal occurrences at the hotel:

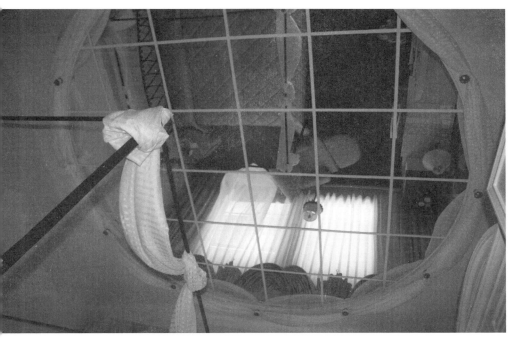

Guests can sleep in the remains of the tank where a worker was eaten by acid!

† **4:30 a.m., June 19**: In the early morning, Sereta would hear noises coming from the back kitchen as if people were throwing dishes around. Another worker came down and they double-checked all the doors, but found no living person.

† **1:32 a.m., July 20**: Chaz heard a big boom in the lobby as if someone had tossed something heavy. Then noises started coming from the kitchen area, as if doors were being jiggled and someone was in the kitchen. Two hours later the boxes next to the back door fell down, scattering themselves on the floor and making a lot of noise.

† **4:02 a.m., July 25**: Chaz heard a loud noise in the lobby near the main doors to the restaurant; she said the clinking sound reminded her of an old metal toy frog that children used to play with.

† **12:57 a.m., August 7**: Chaz heard a man whistling; the sound seemed to come from the front desk area. No person was around and the whistling went for a spell and then simply stopped.

† **4:10 a.m., August 13**: The night auditor heard squealing sounds coming from the kitchen, as if something was being pushed across the floor. Then a thump at the gallery door was heard. Five minutes later voices were heard, getting louder and louder, and then the clinking of dishes. The kitchen doors banged.

† **4:32 a.m., August 13**: Something else was heard being moved in the kitchen. More voices added to the sound, both male and female.

Port Townsend

Port Townsend is one of Washington State's oldest cities and is well known for its ghosts and other mysteries. Sea serpents add to the mystery and were sited off the coast of this city in 1891 and again in 1904. The historical society promotes a Victorian Festival Cemetery Tour as well as other living history tours. Tours are available both on land and on water to explore these mysteries.

In May 1899, the newspaper ran a story about the dark alleyway behind the offices of Rothschild and Company, local shipbrokers. This disreputable waterfront alley leads to the slips where the docks are tied up. The paper reported:

"Captain William Breeze, a pioneer shipmaster on Puget Sound, claims to have encountered the ghost on several occasions during the dark hours of the night when passing through the alley."

According to Capt. Breeze's statement, the ghost is that of a Chinese with his head split in the center. It appears in the alleyway between the hours of midnight and 1 a.m. The first appearance of the ghost with its ghastly wound caused a thrill of terror to creep through the nervous system of the captain, and he lost no time in making a hasty retreat. Since then he has made several attempts to capture it and has succeeded in getting within reaching distance. When he would attempt to lay his hands on the wraith, it would disappear."

This same ghost was also seen by Night Inspector Bropoy of the Customs Service. "On making his nightly rounds in search of opium smugglers, he has encountered the tomahawked Chinese ghost. Chinese never frequent this alley, as a tradition exists among them that many years ago a Chinaman was murdered there...and his body was thrown into the bay."

The Palace Hotel
1004 Water Street

A lovely hotel located on the main street of Port Townsend, if you ask if they have any ghost stories, the front office manager will show you the file that has been kept for years with details of ghostly occurrences. The building was finished in 1889 as the Captain Tibbals Building with a first floor billiard parlor and the Townsend Tavern. The second and third floors were opened to ladies and today are respectfully named for the ladies who plied their trade there. From 1925 to 1933, the hotel was referred to as the "Palace of the Sweets," which was a nice way of referring to a brothel.

As recently as June 2005, a visitor walking down the main stairway felt "something brush against the back of my neck." When photographs were taken, they revealed the presence of orbs in that area. During the

The Palace Hotel is a Port Townsend hotbed of spooky activity.

June 28, 2009 — COMMENTS
Came here to ghost hunt! Had a great time! Loved it, Can't wait to come back.

June 29th 2009 - First time staying for a birthday present. HAD the best time ever! RAN AROUND this awesome town, explored everything! This hotel is excellent! the staff were so nice + helpful! I definately will be coming back. Hopefully next time, Marie will come out to talk!!! EVP! Thanxs for everything! Rex

Had a wonderful time! Everything was comfortable and relaxing. Didn't see any ghost but there were some spooky moments. —Nicole

Had the best time ever! Such a nice hotel and the staff was wonderful. Thank you for everything. Tanahan

Thanks for the great Gost Hunting locabin! Kelly

Loved our room — loved the hotel loved the town. We'll be back!
Jane

Check out the written reports of guests in the hotel log.

Guests report running into this woman's ghost in the Palace Hotel.

The Palace Hotel is a step into the past — enjoy the journey!

winter months of 2004, a clerk was working at the hotel when a guest came back late in the evening. The woman went upstairs, but returned shortly to tell the desk clerk how nice it was of the hotel to have people in the hallway dressed in period costumes greeting the guests. Since the clerk was working alone that night, she asked what type of costume was being worn, suspecting an intruder. The guest explained that the woman she encountered was dressed in clothing like that of the life-sized painting in the hallway. The clerk smiled and explained to the guest that she must have just met one of the hotel's resident ghosts. At that, the guest immediately left the hotel in the middle of the night to find other, less haunted lodging.

In 2007, a guest told an employee that he was alone in his room and had placed a glass of water on a table. A few minutes later the glass had been emptied and was on the sink in the room. A paranormal research team took a photo on October 13th that shows a circular light in a room mirror. This image can be found at the website www.angelsghosts.com/haunted_hotel_ghost_picture.html.

A young guest (Onna, age 8) had an encounter in Room 9a when the child went to the bathroom. When leaving the bathroom, the child tried to unlock the door, but it would not unlock. The guest was frightened and began to scream until the door unlocked of its own volition. The child also heard singing coming from Room 108 and when they opened the door to the room it was found to be vacant.

In 2006, Carol Burteous captured orbs with a digital camera and EVPs of a male voice in Room #1. In August 2006, in Room #1, a witness (Miss Kitty) saw a possible apparition, which she felt was residual and not an active haunt. She caught the image with her digital camera. At the time there was erratic EMF activity and she had some success with spirit/automatic writing in the room.

Manresa Castle
651 Cleveland Street

Charles Eisenbeis, who was the town's first mayor, constructed this building in 1892 with over thirty rooms. The September 30, 1897 Port Townsend Newspaper carried a dreadful headline "SHOCKING DEATH." Charles Eisenbeis, Jr. had been found dead the night before in the basement of the Baker Block family store. This spectacular hotel has been featured on the TV program "Sightings" and is open to the public, which

Visitors can stay at another haunted hotel in Port Townsend... the Manresa.

This clock hasn't worked for years, but late at night, it chimes mysteriously.

can stay and conduct its own ghost investigations and enjoy a wonderful Sunday Brunch.

Jesuit priests purchased the building in 1928; they renamed the building Manresa Hall and used it as a training college. Legend has it that a monk who resided there committed suicide and that you can hear the rope swinging with his body on some nights. It has also been reported that during the early 1900s a young girl named Kate was staying in Room #306 of the castle when she heard that her fiancé had been lost at sea. She committed suicide by jumping from the third floor. There is supposed to be a portrait of Kate hanging in the lounge. One visitor took a picture and said that there was an image of a woman clothed in turn-of-the-century attire and a bonnet staring out the window towards the ocean. These events cannot be corroborated and another legend maintains that a bartender working at the hotel made up these stories to fascinate and entertain patrons. That story, too, has not been corroborated and it may be that the bartender story is another unfounded legend.

One visitor tells of seeing the image of a boy in what appears to be burnt clothing looking down from the windows at the newly arrived guest, who knew nothing of the fire at the building until she entered the residence. Others have reported seeing an eleven-year-old boy wearing torn brown clothing looking out one of the windows.

In Room 202, guests have reported malfunctioning television sets that turn themselves on or off and the sound of voices in the main room when they are in the bathroom. One guest reported a weight sitting on the bed with him as if pulling up the covers. In Room 204, witnesses have reported items moving by themselves and falling to the floor.

Others report smelling the scent of lavender in the hotel and the sound of spirits whispering to each other in the tower room. In February of 2000, a couple heard footsteps along the hallway that stopped outside their door. When they opened the door, there was no one there. Later on they were rudely awakened by someone pounding on the wall next to their bed, but again, no one was in the area.

Today ghostly singing at night and a broken clock that chimes from time to time has been heard by the desk clerk. The clock has not worked for years. Lights go off and on by themselves and doors open and close. A book was once left in rooms so that guests could record their experiences, but was removed because it scared the guests. Recently, an employee reported that when she was alone in a room a book flew off the shelves as if tossed across the room by an unseen hand. Ghost hunters have found sufficient anomalies in the hotel to warrant further investigation.

Rothschild House
Taylor and Franklin Streets

Built in 1868 on the bluff overlooking Port Townsend Bay, the house is now a State heritage site and museum that is open daily from 11 a.m. to 4 p.m. It is the site of the first settlers' cabin in the area in 1851. Temperature variations and doors that slam shut on their own have been reported.

The Rothschild House is a museum with its own ghost.

The Bead Shop
900 block of Water Street

The Victorian style James and Hastings Building was built in 1889; the ground floor and mezzanine are retail shops, with a large basement and residential units above. The spacious lobby opens to the shops that include The Bead Shop, a yarn shop, and a wine merchant. The ghostly prankster in The Bead Shop made his presence known in March 2003 and seems to enjoy frightening the shop's owners and is especially fond of the female clerks.

The Port Townsend Bead Shop is across from the Palace and has its own stories!

The spirit also seems to be attracted to red items for some reason. Activity tends to take place in the late evening when the building is quiet in the retail areas and the basement. Windows that were closed are found opened, while windows that were left open are later found closed. Merchandise moves from one display area to another and are tossed about and disordered. Skeins of yarn have been tossed over the railings and unrolled.

The proprietor was working alone in the building late one evening. A chain barrier had been set up across a restricted space. Lois heard the sound of chains being moved and went to investigate. Everything was in order and no one was around. She returned to her work, but heard the noise again and the unmistakable sound of the chain being loudly handled or dropped with the metal links clinking against one another. She checked the barrier and once again found herself alone in the building, which she left shortly afterwards. She now prefers not to work late into the evening.

The spirit seems to enjoy moving things. One day, the staff was looking unsuccessfully for an advertising banner. After a strenuous search turned up nothing, a clerk went to the basement one last time, only to find the banner neatly folded and placed in plain sight on a table by the stairs. The staff was certain that the banner had not been there moments before.

One day as Lois was closing the basement door, with the doorknob in her hand, the knob was pulled out of her hand by an unseen force. The door then slammed shut.

An apparition of a man about fifty-years-old has been seen around the shop, wearing old-fashioned clothing with a white shirt and a black string tie. He was once seen standing at a top floor window, though the floor was uninhabited and unused at the time. The man disappears when his presence is investigated.

Laurel Grove Cemetery

Located on Old Discovery Bay Road, workers at Laurel Grove had been clearing some berry bushes from a gravesite that kept people from reading the head stone. Louise F. used a rubber mat to kneel on as she worked and when she finished clearing the bushes the mat was about ten feet from her and her truck. As she tossed the last remnants of pruning into the truck, she noticed that the mat was floating a foot off the ground with a little whirlwind beneath it. The mat then shot about twenty feet into the air and returned to earth. Louise took that as an acknowledgement of her labor over the neglected grave and said "You're Welcome!" to the spirits.

Another time she was cutting a shrub over a marker and was working with a pair of work gloves with large, flared cuffs. She threw the gloves to the ground to work on her task and when she looked at them again they were in an upright position beside the grave as if they were praying. Louise checked the headstone to find that it was the final resting place of a reverend.

In 2004, while working on some ivy near Enoch Fowler's gravestone, she had a feeling that she should dig deeper, pulling up roots as she went. Perhaps Fowler's deceased wife inspired her, but after digging on the ivy and pulling up roots, she found the gravestone of Mary Caines Fowler buried eight inches below the soil. Mary Caines Fowler was a pioneer of the region in 1853. Louise greeted the discovery of her long-lost headstone by saying, "Welcome back, Mrs. Fowler!"

Haunted Houses

† A house on Lincoln Street, near Lizzie's Bed and Breakfast, was built in the early 1900s. A family living there from 1986 to 1991 would hear bumps and thumps coming from the attic. When they investigated, they found that items had been shoved around…even though no one had been in the attic. At other times they would hear low, muffled voices of people talking when no one was present. Within a few weeks of moving into the house, their young son mentioned a "boy" that he was playing with. The son would speak and play with the playmate that was invisible to the parents. This continued for six months.

~~~

† Near Jolie Way, a resident, who identified herself as Katie, was walking outside along the dirt road near her house. She felt a tingling sensation and felt the air around her get colder than it had been just a moment before. She used her flashlight to look around, sensing that someone was watching her. There were no people or cars in the area. Then, a light appeared before her about thirty feet away. Katie was frozen with surprise as she watched the light bob up and down as if someone was walking very slowly or hobbling along the road holding a lantern. She ran a bit up the street, stopped, and looked back to find that the mysterious light had vanished as quickly as it had appeared. When she explained this event to her mother, she mentioned that she had a mental impression of an old man in his 70's or 80's. Her mother informed her that an elderly man had once lived alone in a rustic shack on some wooded land nearby. The man died of a heart attack in 1994, but his body was not discovered until a neighbor stopped by a month later.

~~~

† A house at 1924 Holcomb Street was built in 1879. When new residents moved in, they cleaned the dirt floor area below the washer and dryer by raking the soil beneath the deck that the machines stood on. One day the husband asked his wife why she had put a dish on the dirt floor. She didn't know what he was talking about and investigated—and

found a clear bowl with water sitting in the center of the floor. Although they did not have a cat, it seemed to be the kind of bowl one would set out for a cat. There were no paw or footprints in the dirt and the bowl was not one that they owned or had ever seen. This occurred when the doors were locked and no one could have gained entrance.

Animals in the house have been known to behave strangely, barking into space as if they see something. The animals then look at their owners as if to say "Can't you see what I'm barking at?"

One summer afternoon the wife was walking in an upstairs hallway when she felt a cool breeze and saw a brief shadow go past. This may be the same spirit that left the toilet seat up in the guest bedroom when the wife was the only one in the house and had put the seat down earlier in the day.

The ghosts seem to be delightfully friendly and the family living there enjoys their presence. Others have commented on the nice feeling that the house has to it and the spirits even seem to enjoy the husband's music, humming the tunes after the band has finished practicing for the evening. Love may have endured in this home for the past century — and will do so for centuries to come!

Fort Worden

Fort Worden overlooks Port Townsend and is currently a campsite, hostel, and conference center run by the state, which acquired it from the federal government. The fort has a rich military history and is in excellent condition — and a good place to catch ghostly activity, namely orbs.

Photographers can have a certain amount of success capturing orbs and ghosts. Some hot spots to check out are the Guardhouse, the tree in front of the Guardhouse, dormitories 201, 202, and 203, Alexander's Castle, the battery near the castle, and the schoolhouse.

Photographs of housing units and the parade grounds show orbs and, on at least one occasion, the blue image of a man in front of a housing unit was observed. Further investigation is warranted for the guardhouse, parade grounds, and housing units. Check the ghostly images at www.aisling.net/artfest/04/ghosts.html.

Post Military Cemetery

The Post Military Cemetery is located down the road from the guardhouse/information center at the edge of the fort's property. Go past the blimp hangar on the left and the campgrounds on the right; the cemetery is at the end of the road on the left. It is an old military cemetery with tidy white grave markers that is still managed by the Federal mortuary service at Fort Lewis. Some psychics' sense odd feelings in the woods next to the cemetery and in the evening hours it is a great place to get photographs of orbs. Keep the camera stationary, perhaps use a tripod, and take a series of twenty or so pictures. One photographer did this and was rewarded with images of dozens of orbs that seemed to float around the graveyard as the images moved from one shot to another. These orbs were not visible during the shoot — they only showed up on the pictures.

The Guardhouse

According to local legend, a guard accidentally shot himself in the guardhouse — now the information/gift shop — when the fort was active. The soldier is reported to be still on guard duty long after his death. People have reported seeing "sparkles" in the guardhouse, but these sparkles do not appear on film. The "sparkles" are colorful and some are rather large, perhaps the size of a baseball. This anomaly seems to respond to voice introductions by an investigator, resulting in a display. Many orbs are photographed at the guard building. An image of a blue apparition taken there can be viewed at www.hollowhill.com.

The guardhouse is haunted by a sentry who shot himself in the head!

Officers Row

On Officers Row, ghosts have been spotted in the original commander's house on the corner overlooking the water. The duplex buildings are numbered and the westernmost address of each building is noted with the letter W, easternmost with E for East. Researchers may want to start at the end of the street nearest the water at the Commanding Officer's house. The photo of an apparition in that house was featured in an August 2005 Port Townsend Leader newspaper article. The building was constructed in the early 1900s and the smell of burning coal, hot burning sulphur, or burning rubber has been reported near the floor along a doorway, though maintenance workers cannot find the source.

Building 5W on Officers Row has had doors and windows open and close on their own accord.

The current buildings that occupy the area on the side of the parade field across from Officers Row were originally barracks for the enlisted men.

People report seeing spirits in the upper windows of this house when no one is there.

Another haunted house on Fort Worden!

Building 11W used to be officers quarters. A woman was staying overnight and in the middle of the night woke up to feel a presence in her bedroom. She felt a cold wave pass over her body from beneath the covers that were covering her.

From the 1950s to the 1970s, the upper part of the fort was used as a State reform school. Building 201 held the detention cells for the particularly unruly residents and seems to be a popular spot for ghosts to hang out. The buildings are now dormitories.

An undisclosed two-bedroom NCO quarters with two baths was being occupied by an elderly couple and in the evenings they retired to their queen-sized bed. The wife was awakened when she felt something sit on the edge of the bed. Her husband was laying on the other side of the bed, sound asleep.

Alexander's Castle is on Fort Worden... a tale of unrequited love!

Alexander's Castle

Dominating the Fort Worden hillside close to a firing battery position, Alexander's Castle is a castle-looking structure built before the Fort was established. John Alexander was the rector of St. Paul Episcopal Church in 1882 and he built this home to serve as a residence for his intended bride who was still in Scotland. When he traveled to Scotland to pick her up, he found her married to another man. The castle, designed to catch rainwater, is the oldest structure on Fort Worden and has been used as a residence, a tailor shop, and an artillery observation post. Ghostly orbs have been photographed around the castle and sounds have been heard within the building when no one is inside.

PROSSER

Whitstran is a hill along the canal and is called "Gravity Hill" because if a car is in neutral it will roll uphill and powder on the car may reveal fingerprints. Some people report seeing the face of a girl inches away from the person's face inside a truck. The face was an outline of eyes with long black hair over her face as if she had come out of a canal or water. At the time of the report, the canal was dry.

In another instance, a student observed a woman with long black hair jump into the canal off of a little bridge that crosses the canal. Students at the hill turned off their ignitions of their cars and their cars began to move. When they looked back, they reported seeing a young woman who was trying to push the car, as if she wanted them to leave. Rumor has it that in a barn near gravity hill some girls were raped and killed.

PUYALLUP

Meeker Mansion
312 Spring Street

Ezra Meeker built the seventeen-room Victorian Meeker Mansion in 1887. Ghostly activity includes orbs caught on film. One investigation group caught on film a spectral image in one of the mirrors hanging on the wall. Some say that the spirits may be Ezra and his wife, while others have reported a small child that seems to be wandering the halls curiously watching the visitors.

Ezra was an early pioneer of the Northwest, having crossed the Oregon Trail three times by wagon, once by train, once by automobile, and finally, in 1924 in a biplane. He authored many books about the Oregon Trail, including The Old Oregon Trail. Ezra passed away in 1928 at the age of ninety-seven. The home is listed on the National Register of Historic Sites and is now a museum run by the Ezra Meeker Historical Society.

The Meekers' apparently never left their mansion, even in death.

RENTON

Maple Valley Highway

A very dangerous and dark road, many accidents have occurred on this highway. Witnesses have reported driving the road late at night and experiencing an unexplained fog. Immediately after passing through the fog, they report seeing a crying teenage girl standing alongside the road. She appears to be looking for a locket that she lost in the car accident that stole her life.

Along Maple Valley Highway, there is an old deserted haunted house where lights go off and on by themselves...even though there hasn't been electrical service in the house for years.

Renton High School
400 South 2nd Street

Legend has it that a janitor raped and murdered a girl and then hanged her body from the rafters in the old auditorium. She would make herself known only to small groups, as she would play the piano, turn off the lights, and sometimes manifest in the balcony. She is said to haunt the fourth floor and the tower, which is now off limits to students.

McClendon's Hardware Store
440 Rainier Avenue South

Formerly the old K-Mart store, McClendon's Hardware started its existence as the Renton Hospital. It's no wonder then that workers there report mysterious activity in the evenings.

ROSLYN

This picturesque town reminds visitors of the days when coal was "King" and the miners worked in the pits to bring forth the black treasure from the bowels of the earth. While the last mine closed in 1963, the town retains the charm of an old mining community and has a monument to the fallen miners in the downtown area. The vintage charm of this town explains why it was chosen as the movie setting for the hit television series "Northern Exposure."

Roslyn is most noted for its part in a television show about Alaska, "Northern Exposure."

Brick Tavern
1 Pennsylvania Avenue

Investigators claim to feel a presence in the basement of this tavern. Noises are often heard around closing time and some people have reported seeing an apparition of a lost miner.

Bartenders will tell of hearing children's voices in the basement, and ghostly images have been seen in cowboy attire in the pub. Some have gone so far as to explain that if you put a shot at the end of the bar the ghost will leave you alone.

The building was rumored to be a jailhouse for criminals and the cells were in the basement, but these may be simply movie props since in the 1970s jail cells were built in the Brick Tavern for the movie "The Runner Stumbles," starring Dick Van Dyke.

The Brick Tavern is visited by an old miner from time to time.

The Brick Tavern is a warm pub... just mind the spirits!

The Capitol Theatre
101 Dakota Avenue

The ghost of an old stagehand is believed to haunt the Capitol Theatre. Electrical devices don't work correctly; it's as if they are being influenced by temporal beings. People report cold spots in the building that cannot be explained, as well as doors that open on their own.

A former stagehand haunts this old theater in Roslyn, also known as the Capitol Theatre.

The Federal Building

In the William O. Douglas Federal Building, located on Pennsylvania Avenue in the main part of Roslyn, invisible footsteps have been heard on the upper floors. When people hear the heavy footfalls, they go to confront the intruder and find that no one is there.

Other Roslyn Haunts

† The former radio station, KNDX Radio, was said to be haunted by an invisible ghost.

† The Police station is built on the site of an old Armory. People have reported hearing the sounds of soldiers performing drills and marching around the area, but when they look for them they cannot find the reason for the sounds.

SAN JUAN ISLANDS

These islands are key to the development of the Pacific Northwest and can be reached from Bellingham or Anacortes. They include Orcas Island, Friday Harbor, and Roche Harbor.

Roche Harbor Resort
1400 Rosario Way, Orcas Island

Built by Robert Moran, who purchased 7,000 acres of Orcas Island in 1904, the fifty-four-room Roche Harbor Resort began its existence as Moran's retirement mansion, Rosario. Moran later donated 5,000 acres of Orcas Island to the state, which used the land to create the Moran State Park. In 1938, Moran sold the mansion to Donald and Alice Rheem, who had made their millions with the invention of the Rheem Hot Water Heater. This eccentric couple enjoyed life to its fullest, and Alice loved her Harley Davidson motorcycle. She was known to ride her motorcycle to the general store to play cards with the locals. Sometimes she would ride her Harley wearing a red nightgown. The locals told rumors of Alice's wild affairs that she had in the mansion while her husband was out of town.

In the 1960s, the resort was sold and the new owners made additions to the mansion, which boasts guest rooms and a conference center. Employees of the resort have seen Alice on the grounds, although her ghostly activity seems to be restricted to the main building. Strange shadows and shapes have been reported in the evening hours. In the 1980s, one employee was spending the night alone in one of the rooms when she saw the shadow of someone in the room with her. When she turned on the light, the shadow remained and even moved across the wall, as if it cast by a spectral being that was approaching her. She watched the shadow, but looked around to see that she was alone in the room. When she felt invisible hands caress hers at about midnight, she decided to leave. About this same time another couple reported that they heard loud sounds as if a couple was making love in the empty room next to theirs. Both events were reported to the desk clerk that night.

Other witnesses have seen Alice on the second or third floor wearing a red dress in the style of the 1930s. Others have reported hearing a woman in heels walk across the hardwood floors when no one is in the room. Some have reported seeing a woman driving through the second floor on a motorcycle. Shadows, motorcycles in the hall, sounds, and soft touches accompany the practical jokes that the spirits share with their human hosts. The spirits commonly fill the water buckets to overflowing, much to the consternation and annoyance of the housekeeping staff. Perhaps Alice is enjoying her afterlife as much as she enjoyed life.

Roche Harbor Cemetery

There is a mausoleum by the cemetery in Roche Harbor. There are stories that on nights of a full moon, via the long trail leading to it, you can walk up to the mausoleum and see the spirits of the six people who are buried under the seats around the table, sitting there laughing and talking. It is also reputed that when it is raining you can sit at the table and, even though there is an opening in the roof of the mausoleum, no rain will come in. Please note that this is a private cemetery.

SeaTac

The Radisson Hotel was located at 17001 Pacific Highway (Highway 99) at the southwest corner of Highway 99 and 170th Street. Across 170th Street, to the north, is the Washington Memorial Park Cemetery. This hotel was built over part of the Washington Memorial Cemetery and it was said that the bodies were never removed from the property. Only the headstones were moved. As a result, the ghosts of the people who were left under the hotel made an appearance in a certain wing of the hotel.

Ghost hunters were successful in getting EMF readings and capturing orbs on their cameras while the hotel was still there. Activity seemed to be prominent in the wing of the hotel closest to the present cemetery, with guests often hearing people talking outside their doors. Yet, when they went to investigate, they saw no one in the halls.

Time has changed the use of the land, as it is now part of the elevated train to the airport and an elevated truss work for the mass transit light rail system for the City of Seattle stands where the ghostly activity took place. Close examination of the line of pine trees at the west end of the property reveals the same type and age of trees that stand across the street in the cemetery.

SEDRO WOOLLEY

The Sedro Wooley-Curlew Cascade Job Corps was formerly the Northern State Hospital. The Curlew Job Corps location was a former SAC radar base, and a hill nearby is referred to as the "radar hill" since the equipment is still there. This may account for some of the tales of a haunted tunnel, since the Air Force would have used an underground tunnel to man this type of station.

The Job Corps also sits on cherished Native American land and perhaps the spirits interceded with the Job Corps students to help them recover from their past experiences in what was once an insane asylum that operated from 1912 to about 1970. Locally referred to as the Northern State Hospital for the Insane, it was the first institution to do a frontal lobotomy. Shadows have been reported in the dormitory rooms and some people get the feeling of being suffocated in them. There are supposedly over 1,000 unmarked graves in the back and the County has admitted that there were some burials at that location. Mischievous spirits have caused pans to fly off racks and lights to go off and on.

SKYKOMISH

Skykomish Hotel is home of the "blue lady." During the railroad boom, the top floor was a speakeasy and gambling parlor, where ladies of the evening entertained their guests. One of the prostitutes' new boyfriends walked in on her as she was conducting business. The boyfriend had forgotten what her line of business was and killed her in a fit of rage in Room 32. Some say the ghost of the prostitute, Rose, haunts the upper floor. Others say the ghost is Mary, who worked there in the 1920s.

A former fire chief of Skykomish owned the property and reported that when he was doing some repairs in the third-floor bathroom he saw an image of a ghost in a white negligee go past the door. On two separate occasions, when he was alone in the hotel, she followed him down the stairs. Another time she unlocked the door of Room 32 and turned on the light.

This old hotel has been unused for some time with a quilt shop on the lower floor. Occasionally a restaurant will operate on the ground floor. The upper floors are for guests and it is reported that Room 19 is especially active. Some reports indicate that there may be more than one ghost here, and that "some of the old gals are still plying their trade." The rooms appear to have been re-numbered through the years, so it is difficult to determine what room the investigator was in when the incidents were reported.

On the second floor, unexplained cool breezes and Tri-Field EMF spikes were found. One set of investigators managed to communicate with the spirits using the EMF detector, asking questions of the ghost and having the ghost respond with one spike for yes, two spikes for no. Two antique lamps on the ground floor were unplugged, but still demonstrated EMF spikes, despite the fact that there was no electricity nearby. Room 19 seemed to be "EVP Central" with many EVPs captured. Recordings of a male voice saying "hello" or "help," along with "no" and rapping sounds, are heard. Room 14 had some activity that was strong enough to set off motion detectors. Orbs were photographed in Room 33, the ballroom, and the front entrance. An anomalous light near the rear window of Room 3 could not be explained.

Hotel Skykomish in its heyday...

A prostitute was killed by her boyfriend in this Skykomish hotel — and she still haunts the place today!

SNOHOMISH

Cabbage Patch Restaurant
111 Avenue A

The tragic story behind this site is that of a nine-year-old girl who is said to have fallen to her death down a flight of stairs inside the building. According to some reports, she still walks up and down the stairs.

The Cabbage Patch Restaurant... the spirit of a little girl who fell down the stairs to her death is still here!

Oxford Saloon
913 First Street

This used to be an old saloon complete with ladies of the evening. There are three main bars in this building, which is over 110 years old, and are family friendly until 9 p.m. They all serve good food.

The worn wooden floors and antique bar make it a good place to soak up the atmosphere. A framed photograph of an old-time policeman, in a Keystone Cops style uniform, is by the stairs. Officer Henry was killed in a bar fight on the main floor of the restaurant and is now said to inhabit the downstairs ladies' room. He has been seen throughout the restaurant, with witnesses identifying him by pointing to the framed picture and saying, "That's him."

The Oxford... ghosts are just part of the show here!

The inside of the Oxford with its turn-of-the-century bar. Note the doll at the top of the bar.

A former house madam has been sensed hanging around as well, as has a former bar owner who has been known to "slap a few fannies" or make things fly off the countertop. Kathleen is the name of another resident spirit and she appears to be a friendly ghost. She is seen dressed in a beautiful colonial dress in the pub and on the main floor. A woman matching Kathleen's description asked a worker for an Oxford Tavern t-shirt and, when the worker turned away to get it, the woman vanished! She has also been seen in the upstairs area that once housed the brothel.

Psychics have reported sensing other spirits of working girls and a "john" from the old days when a brothel occupied the third floor. It seems that there are up to twenty spirits residing here outside of those known as Johnny Walker and his friend Jim Beam. Ask anyone working behind the bar for a list of the hauntings that have been compiled by visiting psychics or talk to Andrea, the owner, who welcomes visitors to come by and chat. She will tell you about the doll that sits on top of the bar. Every once in a while the doll is sold...only to be brought back for mysterious reasons.

   Andrea will also tell you about the old woman's picture at the back of the bar that doesn't seem to want to be moved. When it's moved to the front of the bar, strange, mysterious events occur until the picture is placed back in its original position. No one knows who the old lady is, so maybe you can shed some light on her! There is also an old bearded man in spirit form that follows people upstairs from the pub below. Andrea will be happy to share stories with you, as well as dispense other spirits for your benefit!

No one knows who this woman is, but don't move her picture!!!

Snohomish Public Library
311 Maple Avenue

The library was built in the early 1900s. The first librarian died of unknown causes and her gravesite is unmarked in a Seattle cemetery. People say they see her ghost walking around in the basement of the library where she spent the happiest days of her life. Many workers hear her footsteps downstairs after hours and some claim to have seen the ghost of Miss McMurchy. Investigators feel that Miss McMurchy remains in the library because she is upset and heartbroken over being fired or laid off the job. She didn't want to leave—and apparently she has not! For a long time the library even kept a live web cam on so that investigators could search for the ghost of Ms. McMurchy by Internet!

SPANAWAY

At Spanaway Lake Park, it is said that children who have drowned in the lake can be heard playing in the playground above the park at night when the park is closed. A fisherman reported seeing the pale corpse of a missing girl who drowned floating four feet under water on the south side of the lake in the early morning. It has also been reported that a teenager was murdered in Spanaway Park.

SPOKANE

Cameo Catering Event Facility
1017 West 1st Avenue

Used as a Masonic Hall for a number of years, mysterious noises are heard and levitations of assorted objects are seen, primarily in the basement of this building. Men are heard talking when the building is empty. It is assumed that members of the Masonic order who have since died object to "guests" in the building, as their rites were secret.

Fairchild Air Force Base
6 West Castle Street

Investigators will find at this Base a KC-135 type tanker aircraft that is supposedly haunted by two people who died on it in flight. Reports persist of strange groaning, loss of power for short periods of time, and objects dropping from their secured points. Fuel leaks come and go.

In the weapons storage area, a ghost called "The Goat Man" has been seen by Security guards.

In the Geiger Corrections Center, a scream was recorded on tape as an EVP in an empty floor; no one heard the scream in person...

Gonzaga Prep High School
East 1224 Euclid Avenue

This high school prepares students to enter Gonzaga University and was started in 1887 by the Jesuits of the Rocky Mountain Mission. The school has been at its present location since 1954.

Prior to 1975, it was an all-boy prep school and a football player had made arrangements for his girlfriend to sneak into the school. She hid in a trap door in a small tunnel underground that led to the furnace. The poor girl snuck into the school, found the trap door, and waited for her boyfriend. Sometime thereafter, the furnace started up and she was burned against the wall of the tunnel. When her boyfriend arrived and opened the trap door, he was not met by his girlfriend, but by the odor of burnt human flesh that wafted up from the tunnel.

It is said that the teenage girl still haunts the halls of the school. Doors in the downstairs hallway have opened by themselves when they are left unlocked and the whispers of a teenage girl can be heard from time to time. One student wrote a story about a girl who died in a tunnel long before she heard the historical account. Perhaps the dead girl was trying to reveal her story of a lost love.

Mead Middle School
302 West Hastings Road

This is the location where people smell stale whiskey and muttering voices can be heard. Doors leading to the outside open by themselves. The story is that a Scotsman who was known for drinking whiskey on the job fell off a ladder and died in the 1930s.

Mirabeau Park Hotel
1100 North Sullivan Road
Spokane Valley

Formerly the Valley Doubletree, employees have been witness to ghostly encounters of a frightening nature. A ghostly woman and her two children have the run of the hotel and cause mischief in different rooms.

The staff avoids one of the rooms close to the front desk, as it has been reported that a man committed suicide in that room. On the third floor there is a ghostly gentleman towards the back that asks staff for fresh towels in a friendly manner, but the man is gone before the staff can get a room number from him.

Monaghan Hall, Gonzaga University
502 East Boone Avenue

This hall is the music building for the University. The structure used to be the private residence for James Monaghan. Many strange occurrences have happened within, including the organ being played when no one is there and various musical instruments playing by themselves. People hear the haunting music some of the time. The culprit is believed to be the ghost of Mr. Monaghan himself. Strangely enough, the music most often heard is the song that was played at Monaghan's funeral.

Growling noises and other unseen forces also make themselves known to unsuspecting individuals. In the 1970s, Father Leedale performed an exorcism to clear the building. It was obviously done in vain, because the haunting still occurs.

Patsey Clark's Restaurant
2208 West 2nd Avenue

This old mansion is now a high class eatery. Employees have reported three ghosts in the wine cellar and say that they throw objects across the room. The spirits seem to be particularly fond of wine bottles.

St. Xavier's Church and School
505 East Providence Avenue

Established in 1909, at this building the face of a dead nun has been reportedly seen in one of the windows. The nun appears to be standing with her face over a candle and screaming.

Other Spokane Haunts

Bowdish Middle School
People see a blurry dark figure in a women's bathroom by the cafeteria. A figure has also been seen roaming the halls between noon and 5 p.m.

Carlyle Care Center
People have reported seeing shadowy figures and experiencing multiple electronic disturbances. One woman reported hearing a little girl's laughter.

Centennial Middle School
Formerly the Park Junior High School, students have witnessed an old woman — *with no legs* — floating around the library. There is also supposedly a man and a young woman hanging from the ceiling at the school's side entrance.

Civic Theater

Opened in 1967, this theater has a resident ghost known as "George." With the electricity off and the lighting booth empty, a spotlight has been known to sweep across the stage. George has also been known to flush the toilets when no one is around.

Double Tree Hotel

Every night since Halloween 1998, a mysterious noise occurs from the fifteenth floor. People have also seen mysterious shadows at this hotel.

At Home, Heart, and Friends

An older woman wearing a long gray dress from the 1900s has been seen walking up and down the staircase in this gift shop.

Northwest Christian Colbert Campus

Some ghost hunters have identified the ghost haunting this campus as "Mr. Altmeyer"; reportedly, he will tell students to leave. Many mysterious occurrences have also happened here.

STANWOOD

Stanwood Museum
27108 102nd Avenue Northwest

People driving by this museum at the intersection of Camano Street and Old Pacific Highway late at night have reported that the curtain in a window gets pulled back, even though the museum is empty at night. When they stop to look, the curtain returns to its normal place. Others have reported seeing a candle being lit.

Pioneer Cemetery
23800 104th Avenue

A black figure has been reported towards the back of this cemetery near a tree overlooking a memorial like headstone. The specter will break a tree branch about six inches thick and chase visitors.

Families that live around there have experienced strange happenings and sightings, and have seen lanterns in the graveyard being held by unknown persons. Others have experienced the lanterns in their own yards, displaying a kind of light show. When people investigate, the lights remain in place for a moment and then start moving towards the investigators before disappearing.

Steilacoom

Steilacoom was founded by Lafayette Balch and is Washington's oldest port and one of the first unincorporated towns in the state. During a fierce December storm in 1862, Lafayette's brother, Albert, was found dead in the woods. Mysteriously, he was half naked and his lifeless body was found laying across the road that leads to Olympia. There were no obvious wounds, but an ax was gripped tightly in the hands of the corpse.

J. W. Bates was a slow-witted resident of Steilacoom who had a prized cow that went missing in 1863. While Bates was searching the city for his cow, one practical joker told him that he had seen the head of the cow impaled on a pike at Andre Byrd's slaughterhouse. When confronted with this falsehood, Mr. Byrd suggested that Bates continue his search elsewhere. Bates became incensed and made threats against Byrd, and on January 21, 1863, ambushed Byrd as he came to town to check his mail at the post office. Byrd was shot in the torso and leg and Bates was arrested.

A day later, just before he died, Byrd defended Bates, saying, "Don't do anything to that man. He's a little retarded." The local lynch mob didn't heed his advice and 150 residents stormed the jail, threw a rope around Bates neck, dragged him to a barn, and lynched him. They left the body hanging from a pole outside the barn until the next day. Some say that under the light of the moon people can see the ghost of Mr. Bates wandering around Steilacoom searching for his lost cow. It seems that when there is a bright moon to light the way for him, apparitions of Bates with a noose around his neck can be seen near Steilacoom Lake and in town near the location of the old jail or saloons, dragging a lead rope behind him.

E. R. Rogers Mansion
1702 Commercial Street

Built in 1891 and now housing law offices, the mansion overlooks Puget Sound. E. R. Rogers built it for his wife Catherine and his daughter, Kate. The financial crisis during the crash of 1893 forced him to move his family to the modest house next door. The Herman family bought the house and operated a bed and breakfast in the mansion during the depression. Historians have said that a local Indian man was hanged from the tree in the corner of the yard.

Many employees have reported mysterious thumping sounds and ringing bells as part of the abnormal occurrences in the building. It is said that one of the owner's wives killed herself in the mansion and still haunts it. Others claim that there is more than one spirit dwelling inside. Electrical problems are common and small appliances turn themselves off and on in the dining and bar area. Employees who enter the attic have detected a heavy smell of perfume that seems to permeate the room. One bartender locked the bar after turning out the lights. Once outside, he looked back to see someone inside the bar, where the lights were on again. The police responded to his call with a K-9 unit, but could find no living person. When they tried to get the dog to check the attic, the animal refused to go upstairs. A disembodied face has been reported in the branches of a tree in the corner of the yard that appears to shine in the dark night. It is not uncommon for cleaning crews who work at night to quit and refuse to come back, stating that the reason they are leaving is that the building is haunted.

Witnesses report seeing vanishing shapes turn doorknobs and feeling a chill in the air. Doors swing open by themselves at night and lights flash on and candles are snuffed out when the smell of cheap perfume permeates an otherwise empty room. Television sets, blenders, and the sound system go on and off and switch channels by themselves.

One patron was visiting from England and was engaged in conversation with some friends at the bar. All at once he dropped out of the conversation and his face went pale as he watched the foot of a woman wearing stockings step through the air and rise into the attic. Perhaps the ghost is that of Kate, who feels she deserved the house in life and will remain there in the afterlife. Or it could be the spirit of a Native American who shows the image of a face illuminated in the tree at the southwest corner of the yard.

The ER Rogers house has a host of electrical problems and dogs that will not go into the attic!

The ER Rogers House was loved by Catherine…. She has never left!

Fairy Pier

The Fairy Pier is the scene where one may catch a glimpse of a young child playing. As one gets closer, the ghostly child changes in appearance into an older and feeble visage that eventually fades away.

On the train tracks in front of the pier, visitors report a faint phantom train whistle. The whistle is supposed to be followed by a scream of someone who was struck by a train long ago.

The Bair Restaurant
1702 Commercial Street

Located on Lafayette Street since the 1800s, this building was once the town post office. It also served as the drugstore and soda fountain in the center of Steilacoom. In the 1970s, the Bair family deeded this central point of town to the local historical museum, which now operates it as a museum and restaurant. Some feel that Mr. Bair never left his beloved drugstore. In the kitchen, ovens set at 350 degrees to bake pies and cinnamon buns are found smoking after twenty minutes and the baker discovers that some unearthly hand has moved the thermostat to five hundred degrees. Dishwashing machines have their wires frayed from the inside out and the hand mixer is constantly being moved around by some spirit. Many employees report having their name being called by a woman's voice when they are alone in the restaurant.

On a regular basis, the restaurant workers will hear ghostly chatter at about 7 p.m. as the spirits gather for dinner in this haunted restaurant.

Several people have witnessed this activity, which lasts about one hour. Tables and chairs move on their own and the apparition of a female ghost has been seen in the kitchen and bathroom areas.

Ghost hunters have captured the image of the former owner, W. L. Bair, in photographs. In the kitchen, utensils would vanish only to turn up in strange places across the store. Customers and employees have witnessed bottle of sauces flying off shelves by invisible forces, including a bottle of salmon sauce, which flew from the top rear shelf of a display five feet to the plank flooring and shattered. During the next three weeks, two other bottles have shared the same fate.

The former owner, Mr. Bair, haunts the Bair Drug and Hardware store.

Washington State Hospital for the Insane

The hospital cemetery is home to over 3,000 former inhabitants who were interred between 1876 and 1953. Since insanity was often a blot on a family's name, the graves were marked with a small stone containing only the patient's identification number.

The hospital was later renamed Western State Hospital. Its most famous resident was the Hollywood actress Frances Farmer. She was treated for schizophrenia with a combination of electroshock therapy and hydrotherapy, where patients are wrapped in a sheet and submerged for hours in a tub of icy water.

The Washington State Hospital for the Insane... Think Fanny Farmer!!!

Frances was a film star who was featured in four films in 1936. By the age of twenty-eight, she had nineteen movies and three Broadway plays under her belt! Her movie starlet tantrums landed her in a courtroom in 1942 and resulted in a six-month jail term. After one night in jail, she was released to a mental ward (shades of Paris Hilton!). From there she went to the Screen Actors Sanitarium in Los Angeles for Insulin Therapy. Half a year later, she was remanded to her parents' custody in West Seattle. After failing to get along with her parents, she was committed to Harborview Hospital for psychiatric evaluation based on an "insanity complaint" by her mother in 1944. King County Courts ordered her to be committed to Western State Hospital and Frances' trip to hell began in earnest. This slide into terror can be explored by watching the 1983 movie "Frances," which starred Jessica Lange as the unfortunate Frances Farmer.

Western State Hospital at that time was overcrowded, with 3,000 patrons and less than twenty doctors to treat them. Farmer claimed that she and other inmates were poisoned, restrained in strait jackets, were tied in sacks, and chained in their padded cells. Riots were frequent in the overcrowded facility and streams of water were shot through thick hoses at the inmates who were often punished by solitary confinement in dark, unheated, tiny rooms the size of small closets. Since Frances had been admitted before, she was considered to be hopelessly insane and housed in the crumbling barracks with leaky roofs, boarded up windows, and rooms that were damp and cold in the winter and stifling hot, insect-plagued in the summer. She and other patients were abused by orderlies and fellow inmates. She claimed that men were smuggled into the women's wards and allowed to rape them.

Ghost hunters have had EMF readings spike in the cemetery, seen wisps of fog that hang low to the ground, circling around the grave markers, and ectoplasm that was invisible to the naked eye has shown up on film. Near the old Western State Sanitarium, when the moon is full and on some rainy, foggy nights, it has been reported that people can hear moans and footsteps in the late night to early morning hours. This is believed to be patients that were once institutionalized there.

The place is in ruins now, but there remains an underground boiler room where most of the sounds are heard. Fire rescue teams have practiced moving around demolished buildings in this area and some of their tie-off's can be seen at the top of some of the concrete buildings that still exist. The fence around the facility shakes for no reason when no one is around and is in such ill repair that it keeps no one out of the area. There have been reports of cold spots, sounds of people, and the cold sense of a presence. Reports include an image of blood on the wall reading "JOE," a handprint, and long dried blood that almost seemed to be dripping.

There is a lake in the woods behind Pierce College on the way to the old Western State Sanitarium. At night and in the early morning hours, you feel a presence, see hazy apparitions, and hear voices. They may belong to a woman who drowned there many years ago.

The site is now the Fort Steilacoom County Park. To get there, follow the signs...

SUMNER

The Grand Central Steakhouse was originally the town's train station. It was converted to a bar and restaurant that hosted illegal gambling and an occasional shooting. Apparitions of ghosts have been seen throughout the building. Disembodied voices have called the living employees by name and glasses have been known to fly off the shelves.

Investigators have taken many photographs of orbs and in one case an investigator asked the orb to move for him. The next picture taken showed that the orb had indeed moved a foot higher from its previous position.

Investigators also reported hearing a ghostly laugh from an invisible man and saw a shadow of a person quickly hide behind one of the booths in the restaurant, although no one was there. Cold drafts are felt around the stage and dance floor that could not be accounted for. Investigators agree that there may be two or three spirits in the building of both sexes.

TACOMA

University of Puget Sound
1500 North Warner Street

University of Puget Sound holds a dubious honor. It is widely believed that serial killer Ted Bundy killed his first victim and dumped her in the foundation of a building being built here. Although her body was never found, people have reported seeing a girl — believed to be her — walking the halls of the building and making strange noises.

Norton Clapp Theater was formerly called the Inside Theatre of the University of Puget Sound and is located in Jones Hall at 1500 North Warner Street. The theater is in the main administration building at the center of campus and is haunted by an unseen, but essentially benign presence. The ghost does not appear physically, but manifests in many ways, including shifting scenery, turning on and off lights, slamming doors, and rattling paint cans. There is one case in which a student was leaning over the catwalk to change a light and lost her balance. She felt an unseen force jerk her backwards onto the catwalk, which kept her from falling.

Did Ted Bundy kill his first victim at the University of Puget Sound?

Tacoma Clock Tower
625 Commerce Street

Built in 1893, this building was used by the city for various purposes, including the mayor's office and police headquarters. During its time as a jail, the basement was referred to as "The Dark Hole" because of the deplorable living conditions for the prisoners held therein. Chimes were added to the tower on Easter Sunday in 1905. In 1959, the building was a prime candidate for demolition, but was saved repeatedly by civic groups, even though the building was largely vacant throughout the 1970s and 1980s. In 1990, the building began a revival of sorts and now houses numerous businesses and foundations. The basement still holds the old jail cells and there are bars on the windows, giving visitors an eerie feeling as they contemplate the square opening in the cell doors where prisoners would get their food. Psychics report bad feelings near and in cells #10 and 11. Investigators have captured orbs in their pictures in this area.

The huge bells have hung in the Tacoma Clock Tower since 1904. The clappers weighed sixty pounds and were connected by rods to the clock mechanism, but have been long since disengaged. Still, some ghostly presence manages to ring the bells sometimes at night. Lights have flickered in empty rooms, alarms are set off by no visible entity, and guards report locked elevators moving by themselves. Other guards have reported seeing shadows that zip around at night as well as the spirit of Mary Lincoln near a display of Lincoln memorabilia in the 1970s and a chair move across a marble floor by itself.

Two women (Barb Bernsten and Gail Ford) ran a restaurant in the Clock Tower

The Tacoma Clock Tower used to hold the old jail cells... the bells still ring!

in 2004. The sisters revived the Clock Tower Restaurant and Bar. Workers reported that the friendly ghost would tug on their apron strings and sometimes toss bowls through the air. On Saturday nights a wine glass or two would sail through the air from some spectral toss. The ghost was referred to as Gus, and would sometimes send dishes flying off the tables as well. In the old restaurant, investigators have been rewarded with photographs of orbs and unusual EMF readings on the main floor as well as in the upper level of the restaurant.

In the upstairs office, where a lawyer shared the space, a magnetic alarm on the door would go off when no one was around, even though the door was locked. The occupants also call the ghost "Gus."

In the Old City Hall section of the Clock Tower, security guards have reported elevators that move on their own accord, lights being turned off and on, and doors that were locked being checked and found unlocked. All of this type of activity occurs when no one is in the area. In the summer of 2009 a sign had been posted on the door of the building saying that the power and water were going to be turned off for non-payment, but if any tenant wanted to pay the bill the power could be restored. I wonder if the elevators will still run by themselves?

Paddy Coynes Irish Pub
815 Pacific Avenue

Down the road from the clock tower is the old Olympus Hotel. Now apartments, the ground floor houses the Paddy Coynes Irish Pub. The basement of this club used to be the Olympus' fine supper club and a worker reportedly committed suicide where an office now is. Pots and pans rattle and mysterious noises are heard at night. One witness reported hearing Patsy Cline singing in the Olympus Hotel.

Does Patsy Cline haunt the old
Olympus Hotel in Tacoma?

Thornewood Castle
8601 North Thorne Lane SW

The deceased builder of the Thornewood Castle, Chester Thorne, has made several appearances over the years. Lights have been turned off when no one else was present and light bulbs unscrewed in his room. Some guests have seen Chester's wife, Anna, sitting in the window seat of her room overlooking the garden. Others claimed to have seen her reflection in her original mirror in the room she occupied, which is now the Bridal Suite. The Thornes' son-in-law shot himself in the gun closet, where his ghost has been seen from time to time. In the old Gentlemen's Smoking Room, light bulbs mysteriously unscrew themselves from their sockets and glass bowls and glasses have been known to shatter when no one is around them.

In the Bridal Suite, young brides have looked at themselves in the mirror only to see the reflection of an older woman standing behind them. When they turn around, no one is there.

People staying in the Gold Room have reported the feeling of being hugged or tucked into bed at night. Footsteps were heard in the empty second floor hallway and some visitors report smelling the tobacco aroma of a vanilla-cherry type of smoke.

Another ghost may be the grandchild of a former owner who drowned in the lake. Occasionally guests will rush down from the Grandview Suite concerned because they see a small child alone by the lake...only to find no child there. People have also reported seeing apparitions in the garden.

A Stephen King miniseries titled "Rose Red" was filmed in Thornewood Castle and aired in February 2002. During filming, the lights in the ballroom came on by themselves. The library scene in that movie was filmed at the Arctic Club in Seattle, another favorite haunt! For more information, visit their website at www.thornewoodcastle.com.

Gog-li-hi-ti Wetlands

Just to the south of Wetlands Park was an old burial ground along the Puyallup River where the Puyallup Indian tribe buried their dead. The Army Corps of Engineers has fenced off the area. Fishermen in the area report seeing Native Americans paddling a canoe — when the paddler pulled up to the bank, the canoe would vanish.

Late at night workers and fishermen have seen the spirit of an old man with a yellow dog walking the banks of North Levee Road. Some people claim to have seen the ghost of a man with an angry expression on his face in the area. Sounds have been reported that cannot be explained, such as the wailing of a dog, human voices, and even singing near the river.

Hollywood on the Flats, located immediately adjacent to the Wetlands, is also known as "Hooverville." The last transient was evicted in 1952. The old transient, wearing a tan shirt and pants, held the Pierce County Sheriff Deputies and Tacoma Police at bay with a shotgun, refusing to leave his "home." The standoff ended with a single gunshot when the man took his own life rather than be evicted. Some people report hearing the wailing of his old yellow mixed breed dog.

Pantagenes Theater
901 Broadway

> Directions from I-5: Take the City Center exit to Highway 705 and follow Highway 705 to the "A" Street exit. From "A" Street, turn left onto South 11th Street. For Park Plaza North Garage, turn right on Commerce Avenue.

Tacoma's Pantagene Theater has a ghost of itself.

Built around 1918 as a vaudeville theater, the building hosted such acts as WC Fields, Mae West, and Charlie Chaplin. It is located near 8th Avenue and Broadway in the Theater District of Tacoma. Part of Tacoma's Broadway Center for the Performing Arts, the theater seats over 1,100 patrons at a time.

It was a theatrical custom to keep a stage light on between shows. This "ghost light" was always illuminated so that thespians wouldn't fall off the stage or through a trap door when they were rehearsing or setting up for the next show. Stagehands have reported seeing a translucent figure on the stage between shows. When they called out to this woman in a long dress, she continued her walk into the wings, where searches proved fruitless. Performers have heard someone knocking on their dressing room doors, but when they open the door, no one is there... perhaps it is the same spirited woman.

The Pantagenes has a face carving that may be the image of Alexander Pantagenes, the theater's founder. It is said that when the ghost of Mr. Pantagenes disapproves of a production, the expression on the carving changes, showing his displeasure.

Ghost hunters have investigated the Pantagenes. They reported documenting EMF field variations and said that a compass spun wildly in the basement beneath the stage.

Point Defiance Park
5605 North Owen Beach Road

The Pagoda
Formerly the trolley terminus at Point Defiance in the early part of the twentieth century, the building now known as the Pagoda was remodeled and is now rented out for weddings and parties. Visitors, workers, and

Tacoma's Pagoda is haunted by a newlywed who shot himself there.

even the police have reported hearing footsteps made with hard-soled shoes walking around the building after dark. The footsteps seem to be walking down the stairs on the east side of the building and then they abruptly stop. Sighing can be heard at other times and there are cold spots in the storage area below the building.

A tale has been told about a young newlywed couple during the 1920s. The husband and wife would catch the trolley to Point Defiance and the husband would see his wife off for the day to visit her parents on Vashon Island. Small groups of boats would shuttle people to the island for a fee. The husband would return in the evening to meet his wife. As the small launch she was riding in approached the Boathouse area, it took on water. Many people were thrown overboard in the confusion and the husband observed with his pocket spyglass his wife flailing in the water in her heavy period clothes as she went under. Overcome with grief, he walked down the stairs to the marbled restroom, pulled out a small pocket pistol, and shot himself in the head. It is said that his ghost haunts the Pagoda.

Lost Little Girl

The locals tell the story that somewhere on 5 Mile Drive in Point Defiance Park a little girl was riding her bicycle in the late 1980s. She was murdered and her killer was never brought to justice. Visitors report hearing the sound of a bicycle on the road late at night. In one instance, a woman was driving on the road after the park was closed. As she rounded the turn near Narrows Viewpoint, she saw what she thought was a young girl with a bicycle standing by the side of the road. When the woman stopped the car, her boyfriend got out of the car to ask the little girl if she was okay. The boyfriend approached the little girl, but was frightened when he saw that she had no eyes. He raced back to the car, screaming at his girlfriend to drive away. As the car sped away, the woman looked in the rearview mirror…and saw that the little girl had vanished.

Puget Sound Mental Hospital
215 South 36th Street

Puget Sound Mental Hospital is a large facility for the mentally disturbed (and a drug and alcohol rehabilitation center). Parts of this eight-story complex are no longer in use. Half of the facility lies in darkness and is used for storage or is closed off because it is "unsafe," but all of the buildings here are highly haunted. Most of the staff are willing to tell tales of the many ghostly personalities that reside there. The most famous is that of an old woman and her walker that can be seen and heard going up and down the hallways of the fourth floor. This place is a working facility; visitors need permission to tour the campus.

Temple Theater
47 Saint Helens Avenue

At this theater, people report hearing sounds of furniture being moved across the floor even when rooms are empty. Doors and windows are closed and later found to be open, and a glowing apparition has been seen in the balcony.

THORP

Visitors to the private Thorp Cemetery (also called Bolster Cemetery) on Thorpe Cemetery Road have reported seeing the ghost of an Indian woman crying by the tombstones in the moonlight. It seems the spirit is of a woman named Suzy who was lynched in the 1890s. She has also been seen riding a white horse.

TOPPENISH

A woman, whom ghost investigators have described as being "weird," and a man haunt the top floor of the Toppenish Public Library and can be seen looking out the window.

The third floor houses a museum; passersby have reported seeing some sort of shining blade through the windows when the building is closed.

VANCOUVER

Fort Vancouver

A trading post of the Hudson's Bay Company, the Fort was the first settlement in the Pacific Northwest. At Fort Vancouver, the ghost of Dr. John McGloughlin still haunts his old house; they say you can hear his heavy footsteps walking up and down the halls. There are also reports of people in the lookout tower that can be seen from the ground.

The old army barracks are still occupied and are a stone's throw from the old Fort Vancouver. It is believed that the barracks were constructed over several old colonial graves — there have been stories of ghosts haunting the auditorium and the officers' housing.

Officers' Row
The Grant House is a part of Officer's Row, a strip of colonial style houses that was used to house officers of the Vancouver Barracks since the mid 1800s. The Grant House was the first one built and was once home to President Ulysses S. Grant during his tenure before his presidency. A former officer named Sully haunts the house...the ghost

is even mentioned in the pamphlet at the front door. The house is now a folk art museum and restaurant.

On Officer's Row, there is a house two lots to the left of the Grant House where visitors report that on Saturday through Tuesday the grass in front of the house is dead and brown. Inside the house there is a substance that looks like blood dripping from the walls. The local newspaper reported that a tenant's wife had spent hours scrubbing the walls, but the blood continues to appear.

Veterans Hospital

The third floor of the old Veterans Hospital used to house mentally disturbed patients. It is said that visitors can still hear their hysterical screams, and any paper brought into the room will float to the ceiling and stick there.

School Gymnasium

Late at night, in the gym of the former Fort Vancouver High School, people report hearing a loud crash resulting from a ladder falling. They also see man falling from what looks like thin air. Upon impact with the ground, there was a loud crack... One teacher reported that when this happened the teacher saw bones poking out of the specter's neck just before he disappeared. According to one rumor, a maintenance man was putting up a basketball hoop in the 1930s when his ladder broke and he fell to his death.

Kiggens Theater
1011 Main Street

The resident ghost at this 1930s style theater has been known to turn lights on and off and his footsteps have been heard when no one else is around. Activity in the projection booth includes flickering lights and switches being reset on the system when no one is present.

Sometimes employees will see a dark figure seated far from the lobby get up, walk to the hallway leading to the lobby, and vanish. Another couple has been seen at the end of a movie when most patrons have left. This non-descript couple seems to be watching the credits on the blank screen, with the man wearing a hat and the woman wearing an old hairstyle. When ushers approach them, the couple simply vanishes.

WATERVILLE

A few miles outside of the town of Waterville there is an old schoolhouse that was built in 1864. The windows are now shattered and boarded up, but passersby have reported seeing candlelight emanating from those old boarded up windows. Flashlights and candles go out when people enter the main room of the schoolhouse.

A swing set used to sit on the site, but it was removed long ago. Still, neighbors claim to have heard children playing in the area even though no children were around...at least not visually. It is said that if you listen intently, you can hear the squeaking of the swing set that has long since been removed.

West Seattle

Kubota Garden
9817 55th Avenue South

Near the intersection of 55th Avenue South and Renton Avenue South, investigators can find Kubota Garden, a large Japanese style garden. It is said that walkers on the path near the house hear strange howling sounds, and at night people report hearing the dead whispering to each other.

West Seattle High School
3000 California Avenue

West Seattle High School is a designated Seattle Landmark, having been built in 1917. In 1924, Rose Higgenbotham was discovered to have hanged herself. The spirit of this former student has been said to roam the halls and ground; "she" can sometimes be seen and photographed staring out the window. In June 2007, an image of Rose was captured on film at 7:30 p.m. as she looked out onto the grounds from an upper window. The image can be found at www.friarslantern.com. The school is closed to visitors during the school season.

Admiral Benbow Inn
4212 SW Admiral Way

Located on Alki Beach, when a former resident had an office upstairs at the inn, she heard footsteps walking around. Assuming there were crows on the roof, she thought nothing of it. As the footsteps got louder, she thought that someone or something was walking on the roof. When she investigated, no one was there. Realizing that it had to be somebody walking around that she wasn't seeing, she paid more attention to the sounds.

As she was working alone in the back where the safe was, she heard somebody out in the hall. Thinking that she had failed to lock the front door and that a customer may have walked in, she called out, "We're not open." When she came out into the hall, she saw a long skirt and black shoes move around the corner. She didn't see a head, but did catch a glimpse of a shoulder. Hurrying to catch up to the specter, she rounded the corner to find that the ghost had disappeared. A search of the back door and alley proved fruitless, though witnesses have also reported seeing the long skirt and legs. But because the head of this specter has never been seen, it is unknown if it she is a young or older woman.

Another time she was working with a cleaning man who asked her to stop turning the restroom water on and off. It seems that he was out front cleaning where the coffee shop was and the water was going on and off all the time. They investigated the bathrooms, but they were empty. Shortly afterwards, the water was heard running again. Then it was turned off. Then on, then off, then on and off and on... The cleaning man asked, "What's going on?" He was informed that there was a ghost in the restaurant that was evidently playing a game. The man was bothered by this fact, finished his job, and left the restaurant in a hurry. One girl who worked at the shop also heard the water turning off and on and claims to have been pushed down the stairs because the ghost didn't like her.

WELLINGTON

One of the greatest railroading catastrophes occurred in Washington when an avalanche swept down on the little town of Wellington. Two trains were waiting for the tracks between Spokane and Seattle to be cleared of snow during the last days of February 1910. The mountains overlooking the rail lines were packed with an unusually thick amount of snow. When the rainstorm lubricated the packed snow, the mass of ice and snow became a deadly time bomb just waiting to be set off. The town of Wellington was isolated on the mountain and its residents had gone to sleep around 11 p.m. Likewise, the train crews did their best to get comfortable and get some sleep. Passengers in the trains — men, women, and children — heading to Seattle on the Great Northern route through Stevens Pass made their way to their beds by midnight. On the first of March, the skies over Stevens Pass became illuminated with lightning as a rare thunderstorm passed over the area. The deep rumbling woke some of the crew and passengers who looked out their windows, nervously viewing their precarious situation.

The avalanche smashed into the railroad tracks and tossed locomotives, rail cars, and people into the frozen valley at 1:42 in the morning of March 1, 1910. Acres of snow and debris rushed towards the trains; by the time it hit the rail line, the avalanche was estimated to be half a mile wide. With over 125 people aboard, rail cars were tossed in the air and then fell into the steep ravine, some spinning wildly, others hurled like a football. Occupants were shot wildly about in the cars while some were tossed outside in the snow, where some were smothered. Others managed to survive in the dismal rain.

The residents of Wellington were awake and responding to the avalanche. Some thought that the trains had merely been knocked off the tracks, but then discovered with horror that they had been tossed into the ravine. Rescuers assembled at the east end of town at the engineers' bunkhouse and began to get organized. The most qualified surgeon on hand happened to be the son of a doctor, and hotel workers assembled razors and medical supplies for the makeshift hospital at the bunkhouse. In the meantime, rescuers were reaching the bottom of the ravine to find the mass of humanity that had been slaughtered by the accident. One baby was found torn in half; another rescuer found a hand, another a head severed from their body by the force of the avalanche. By the afternoon, Ida Starret was pulled out of the wreckage, in deep shock and almost frozen. She would be the last person rescued alive.

Rescue workers had to trek through the mountains to reach the site, since the rail lines were out. For the next sixteen days, they recovered bodies from the wreckage. The official death toll was ninety-six people. The precise number may never be known, as the Great Northern did not keep passenger lists. Transient laborers came and went regularly.

The Great Northern railway built a stronger, concrete snow shelter on the tracks to protect the railway. In October 1910, they renamed the town of Wellington "Tye," erasing the memory of the great disaster in all of their literature as not to concern travelers making their way west. In 1929, a new tunnel was built to bypass the more dangerous one where the accident occurred, leaving the town of Tye (Wellington) alone on a mountainside, the silent reminder of one of America's worst railroad tragedies.

The area is now part of the national forest. When a ghost hunting group asked for permission to camp there, rangers told them of strange sounds reported by other campers, including moaning and metal crashing into metal. Strange lights have also been seen at night in the area between the railroad tracks and the ravine. The investigators were urged not to be in the area after nightfall...people have reported seeing mysterious lights in the now abandoned tunnel. The tunnel is about two miles long and can be walked through by visitors. It's a long, dark journey and it gets cold inside, so investigators should bring jackets, solid walking boots, and flashlights.

WENATCHEE

Cherub Bed & Breakfast Inn
410 North Miller Street

It has been said that a long time ago, at the Cherub Bed & Breakfast Inn, a husband came back from vacation to join his wife. When he arrived, he found his wife cheating on him with another man. The husband killed the other man on the stairs of the Bed and Breakfast. Some say that the sound of footsteps walking up and down the stairs can be heard when no one is there. Bloodstains can be seen on the stairs that disappear for a few moments when washed and then reappear later.

WHITE SWAN

At the old Fort Simco State Park, witnesses have reported seeing a woman looking out one of the back windows of the commanders' house. It is thought that she may be the wife of the commander who died of fever in the 1800s.

The fort may also be the source of the Toppenish ghost lights seen in the area in 1973.

WHITMAN

LaCrosse High School
111 Hill Avenue

The LaCrosse schoolhouse is a location where people feel as if they've been pushed or bumped when they are visiting all by themselves. Visitors have also reported a feeling of being watched, as well as seeing the shadow of a person walking down the hallways hitting the lockers.

WOODINVILLE

Chateau Ste Michelle Winery Manor House
14111 northeast 145th Street

This house is located on 150 beautiful acres of land that Seattle lumber and dairy baron, Fredrick Stimson, previously owned. According to legend, Mr. Stimson managed to get one of the servant girls pregnant. When Mrs. Stimson found out, the servant girl "fell" to her death down a back stairwell that leads to the kitchen.

Security systems have been known to malfunction for no apparent reason. Shadows have been seen, cold spots that seem to follow people have been felt, and noises have been heard. The spirit has also been known to open the upstairs restroom window, close the doors, and turn lights off and on. The cleaning staff has reported hearing, late at night, footsteps when no one is there, as well as toilets flushing.

Yakima

Cherry Park
North 4th Avenue and Cherry Street

People have reported ghostly children running around in circles, screaming at the top of their lungs, hundreds of times at this park. This goes on for a good thirty minutes while a strong scent of sulfur remains in the air.

Yakima Canyon

> Directions: From Seattle, take Interstate 90 east to exit 109; turn left off the exit ramp onto Yakima Canyon Road; drive through Yakima Canyon to Red's Fly Shop. The preserve is adjacent to Red's to the north (upstream). Turn around in Red's parking lot and find a place along the highway shoulder to pull off. In the fall and winter, wade across the shallow side channel out to the island part of the preserve.
>
> † Another way to access the preserve is by boat: Raft the Yakima River from the top of the canyon for an all day excursion, or put in at the Umptanum access area upstream from the preserve. Red's Fly Shop offers rentals.

Located about two miles north of the Roza recreation area, the canyon is supposed to be haunted recently by a young Hispanic male who was murdered there and an elderly man with gray hair and beard who committed suicide in the same area.

St. Paul's School
15 South 12th Avenue

Visitors to the fourth floor of St. Paul's School report hearing a little scream or seeing a little shadow of a very short lady who taught at St. Paul's twenty years ago. This would be Sister Sabiena...it is rumored that she jumped out of a window or died in an elevator.

Sounds have also been heard on the fourth floor when people are on the floor below, though no one is on the floor above. In the girls' bathroom, the sound of flushing toilets and water turning on may be heard, even though no one is there.

Yakima Memorial Hospital
2811 Tieton Drive

Located between 14th and 16th streets, people claim to catch a glimpse of someone or something walking, running, or sitting down at this hospital, but when they turn to see the vision the image vanishes.

Near the morgue people get the feeling that they are being watched, and around the elevator they have experienced cold drafts. People also see the elevator doors opening and closing on their own volition.

ISLAND HAUNTS

Bainbridge Island

Folks on the island talk about the Rose addition part of their community as one that should be left alone after dark. Apparently the specter of a female spirit has been spotted along the road in that area.

Another haunted site is the Messenger House in the Rolling Bay area. This place may have been one of the early hospitals or clinics in the area; people have reported hearing the sound of screaming and seeing images of surgery being performed as if it was an early pioneer day. Others have reported seeing a lady sitting at a lamppost in the area.

Blake Island

This island hosts Seattle's famous Tillicum village, an Indian Longhouse accessible by boat from Seattle's harbor, six miles to the east. Salmon cooked on planks in an open pit make a special evening with the accompanying Indian rituals and dances for over 100,000 annual visitors. The island was the ancestral camping ground of the Suquamish Indian Tribe and legend says that Chief Seattle was born on the island. The island was a great source of timber that was harvested and shipped off to San Francisco when Seattle was being developed.

Few realize that the island was known as Trimble Island when Mr. William Trimble had an estate there from 1903 until 1929. The rambling two-story mansion on the northeast side of the island had five fireplaces on the ground floor, wide verandas, and sleeping porches in this summer home that the family lived in year-round from 1917 to 1923. The family traveled to and from the island on their fifty-foot boat, the Athena. When Mrs. Trimble died in an automobile accident in December 1929 in which her car sank in Elliott Bay, the family was devastated and never returned to the island. The stock market crash of 1929 completed the demise of the Trimble family and Mr. Trimble lived the rest of his days in a small house on Capitol Hill until his death in 1943.

Eventually, the gardens, tennis court, horse pasture, and even the house began to revert to nature. In 1933, bootleggers made some of the finest moonshine (known as "alkee") in the region on the island. When the Trimbles owned the land, their three caretakers would ward off the rumrunners, since Mrs. Trimble had established the island as a bird sanctuary where firearms were prohibited.

When part of the land was sold in 1936, the island became known once again as Blake Island. Vandals and rumrunners camped in the house, tearing up the fancy woodwork for firewood, breaking windows, and generally destroying the place until it was consumed by fire when two high school students left an unattended fire in the fireplace in 1940. Some speculate that there was a murder on the estate before it was turned into ashes.

Today, the island is part of the Washington State Park system with 475 acres of camping and five miles of saltwater beach. Reachable only by boat, there are mooring markers floating off the island so that boaters can tie up and spend the night, and there is a small marina provided by the vendor, Tillicum Village.

The foundation of the Trimble mansion can still be found behind the longhouse. Well-marked trails run on either side of the foundation and the site is marked on park maps (www.parks.wa.gov/maps). Campers can use the campgrounds nearby, or sleep on their boats. Ghost hunters have picked up EVPs and loud sounds of people having a large party accompanied with boisterous laughter has been reported. Sometimes a woman's scream and the crash of lumber can be heard as well, and researchers have heard a man yelling "No, no... No!!" and the crash of lumber as if the roof of an old building had collapsed.

Whidbey Island

Coupeville
† At Sunnyside Cemetery near Ebey's Landing, a headless ghost has been reported there and in an old cabin his family occupied after his death.

~~~

† The one-room schoolhouse near the intersection of Highway 20 and Zylsta Road was built in 1895. It is now used as a rental unit where the ghost of a small girl dressed in period clothing is well known to long-time locals. Some have reported seeing the ghost looking out the window or on the front porch as they drive by. Water faucets will turn on and off by themselves and objects have been known to float during Halloween parties.

Movie crews have had difficulty with their equipment as they tried to film there. They also heard sounds and creaks that kept a scene from being used in the movie "The War of the Roses" with Danny DeVito,

Kathleen Turner, and Michael Douglas. With all the problems on the set, DeVito looked at the building and said it was haunted. They did not return for another shoot.

A later resident was making cookies in her kitchen when she noticed a blond haired boy in the kitchen with her. She turned to get the boy a cookie, thinking that he was a local who had wandered in. When she turned back to hand him the cookie, the lad had vanished. She has heard children mimic the voices on her television set and laughing in the building. One morning she heard boys' voices counting "one...two... three" — and then loudly telling her to wake up. In her sleepiness, she rose and shouted for the children to be quiet. When she looked around the room, she discovered that she was alone in the eerie silence.

~~~

† At Fort Casey, there are strange drawings on the walls and visitors report hearing something scratching on the walls. Figures and a woman screaming have also been reported.

WASHINGTON STATE'S OTHER GHOSTLY SITES

† In Burien, one haunted location is the Lakeside Milam Treatment Center. It's reputed that a young boy hanged himself there... employees have seen his spirit wandering the halls.

† At Lake Stevens, a woman drove through a railing on the road and drowned. People claim to see her spirit floating above the water staring at them as they drive by.

† At McChord Air Force Base, a C-141 transport aircraft was used to transport the bodies of 900 people back from Jonestown, Guyana in South America after Jim Jones, the founder of the religious cult the Peoples Temple, had ordered their suicides. Maintenance personnel report hearing voices and footsteps, and the auxiliary power goes on and off by itself.

† At Washington State University in Pullman, there seems to be a ghost that enjoys living in the dormitories. In Orton Hall, on the fourth floor, students report strange events and the cleaning staff has been known to refuse to go up there.

† In Purdy, it is rumored that in the late 1970s a child was hit by a car on Purdy Bridge. People have reported seeing the image of a child on the bridge. The spirit child seems to be darting across the bridge although his appearance is unpredictable.

† At the Puyallup Fairgrounds, the large Ferris wheel starts going and one of the seats start to rock. Screaming is also heard from time to time.

† In Queets, at the Native American Burial Ground, visitors have reported hearing strange noises resembling the beat of drums and Indian singing.

† At Spanaway Jr. High School, lights flicker and alarms go off.

† The Tokeland Hotel (2964 Kindred Avenue, Tokeland) is haunted by an oriental man, possibly Chinese. Animal spirits of dogs and cats have also been reported at this location.

† In Waitsburg, the Haunted Tunnel in this old-fashioned Walla Walla County town has a ghost. A man walks the tracks holding onto his severed head. Supposedly the machinery that caused his decapitation has been seen following along behind this specter.

† At the Rite-Aid Store in West Seattle, between the Alaska, California, and Morgan junctions, a spirit has been seen visiting the aisles near the personal hygiene products.

Section Two:

HAUNTED CEMETERIES

Chapter Five:

CEMETERY ICONOGRAPHY

MESSAGES FROM THE PAST

From the earliest days of society, mankind has buried their dead. The oldest form of burials date back four to five thousand years B.C., when mourners built a tomb called a Tumulus into rock or earthen hills. These final resting places resembled grottos. In cemeteries, one can find various types of tombs or memorials. A sarcophagus may be found in cemeteries around larger metropolitan areas in America. This is normally aboveground with legs or a round/tapered base. A chest tomb resembles a large container or shipping trunk that has artwork on the outside. An altar tomb resembles an altar used for worship with more ornate artwork on the outside than is found on a chest tomb.

Some markers tell a simple story.

Ancient Egyptians left writing on the walls of their tombs to let people know who was buried inside. Inscriptions told of the accomplishments of the entombed, who they were related to, and the names of their wives and children as a symbol of their importance. The headstones encountered today in a cemetery convey the same purpose.

Headstones mark the ground where people are interred. When walking in a cemetery, one may encounter family members who are visiting the final resting place of those who have passed on. A spouse may leave flowers on a gravestone, pat the stone, or read the comforting words left behind such as "Loving Wife." Human beings have left memorials to mark their passing throughout recorded history. As time goes on, some of the meanings may lose their popularity with modern culture. For example, the swastika was once a popular symbol, but after it was adopted by the Nazi party few used it to adorn the headstones of their loved ones.

Mankind has always formed clubs and organizations around common themes. Some of these organizations continue to thrive, while others may have become extinct. The stones may be adorned with symbols of a culture that has expired. Pictures, drawings, words, and symbols etched in stone provide a glimpse into the accomplishments of the person buried there. Perhaps the person was a member of a fraternal order or professional society. Military personnel are buried in national sites cared for by the government as a tribute to their service.

The messages are still there, but the meaning may have become hidden with the passing of time. The modern visitor to old graveyards can read words that are hundreds of years old. These memorials speak to us about

Edwin died in a swimming accident.

Thomas Youngblood died while serving in the military and is buried at Arlington National Cemetery.

an age gone past. In Arlington Cemetery, a simple white marble marker identifies the military person in our nation's greatest memorial. In other cemeteries one can find more information on the stone. Some are easier to understand, such as the Meehan stone that identifies the deceased as the first person to die in the war as a merchant marine!

Symbolization

The study of symbols on gravestones is called Iconography. It may help efforts to communicate with ancient spirits if you take the time to learn about the person and their accomplishments when the spirit was in the flesh. This section explains the meaning of some of those symbols.

Anchor: Symbolizing hope, it was an early Christian symbol. It refers to Pope Clement, who was tied to an anchor and dropped in the sea to drown. Early Christians used the anchor as a disguised cross, and if the chain on the anchor is broken, it indicates that the ship is no longer bound to earth and is in heaven. An Anchor Cross resembles two upturned anchor ends in the form of a cross that is considered a reception of matters spiritual.

However, today the Anchor also serves to note a person who has served in the navy or maritime.

An anchor tells us that the person was a seafarer... The monument shown here indicates that the man was a fisherman who contributed to his community.

Arrow: Shows the mortality of man.

Books: Often found engraved on markers, the closed book symbolizes a full life in that the departed has fulfilled the last chapter before passing on. It may also represent the Bible. Open books are used to register the names of the deceased. A Bible indicates knowledge or that the deceased was a minister or teacher.

Books indicate the closing of a chapter.

Birds: Symbolizing flight to the hereafter, flying birds also symbolize rebirth. The dove is spotted most often in cemeteries in a wide variety of poses, a symbol of purity and refers to the Holy Ghost. Sometimes it has an olive branch in its beak.

Eagles denote resurrection and rebirth as well as a sign of generosity. It was chosen to represent generosity since the eagle leaves half of its prey for other creatures to feed on. Eagles also indicate courage, faith, generosity, and military service.

Second only to doves in Christian art is the Pelican, which symbolizes the ultimate self sacrifice of a parent's love for the children.

Sometimes the Phoenix can be found on the grave; it represents resurrection, transformation, and rebirth.

Birds symbolize flight to the hereafter.

Bugles: This symbol indicates military service and the resurrection.
Butterflies: Symbolizes an early death, or a life that was short-lived, such as a child's. A Cherub or small chairs also indicates a child's burial site.

Cannons: Designating military service, when found on the base of a stone, it indicates that the person served in the artillery.

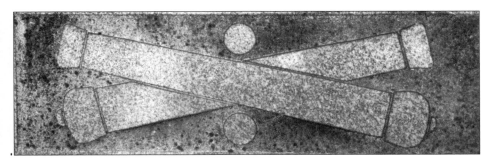

Cannons and crossed sabers indicate military service.

Dogs: In Chinese cemeteries, dogs are said to ward off evil spirits and are guardians of Buddha. Sometimes dogs are depicted as the best friend of the deceased, a partner who played a key role in the life of the person, usually as a devoted companion. Normally a male will be on the east and a female on the west. The ball under the male dog represents the emptiness of the mind and the female often has a baby Shih Tzu under her paw.

Dragons: For the Chinese artist, these creatures are the ultimate highest spiritual party representing natural wisdom and strength.

Eyes: When found on grave markers, eyes are an ancient symbol of God and is usually associated with the Masonic order.

Hands: Clasped hands indicate a farewell and the hope of meeting in eternity, such as the everlasting union of husband and wife. Normally the clasped hands have one masculine and one female arm or sleeve, and hands held together is a symbol of matrimony.

A hand coming down from a cloud with three fingers represents the trinity, while a hand in the upward position indicates that the soul of the departed has reached Heaven. Two fingers pointed upwards indicate that the person was a member of the clergy. A single finger pointing up shows the pathway to heaven, or a heavenly reward.

Clasped hands indicate a farewell.

Praying hands indicate reverence.

Fingers pointing up shows the pathway to heaven.

Lamb: Indicating innocence, the lamb often marks the grave of a child or even a woman's grave. A lamb on a gravestone often represents the innocence of youth or a reference to Christ being the Lamb of God.

A lamb indicates a child is buried here.

Two lambs indicate two children are buried here.

This well-preserved lamb and stone commemorates a lost child.

Lions: Often found at the entrance to cemeteries and graveyards, the Lion denotes majesty, courage, and strength. Stags are symbols of piety and their antlers can also be seen to represent the tree of life.

Open Gates: Symbolizes that the soul is entering heaven or the afterlife.

Ships: On gravestones, it indicates a seafarer who went down with the ship. As a symbol, it may represent the church on its voyage. A broken wheel, however, indicates that the journey is over.

Skeletons: A reclining skeleton represents a passive death, silently waiting for the mortal world to end. A standing skeleton is known as the King of Terrors and is often seen with an arrow, dart, spear, or scythe.

Skulls: A skull with crossed bones indicates the mortality of man, penitence, and the transitory nature of earthly life. Skulls are considered to be the ultimate symbol of death, reminding us all that sooner or later death will take us.

Swords: On graves, they indicate military service, possibly that the person served in the Infantry if the sword is found on the base of the stone. If the sword is upside down, it indicates the relinquishment of power or military service. If sheathed, it means temperance. If swords are crossed, it indicates that the person died in battle.

Urns: Symbolizes immortality, or the death of the body and its return to dust in a final resting place as the soul gains its place in the hereafter. Draped urns are symbolic of the veil between heaven and earth and are common on graves from the nineteenth century.

Community Organizations

Fraternal organizations, societies and clubs often had secret symbols that found their way onto the gravestones. Some of the abbreviations found on tombstones may be so old that their meaning has become faded or forgotten. Yet the organization played a key role in the development and life of the person interred and ghost hunters should understand these hidden meanings.

American Legion (AL)

This group of former servicemen was founded in Paris after World War I in 1919 with a single patriotic goal — help wartime veterans. The group works to provide benefits for servicemen who are injured, wounded, and elderly. There are over three million members in over 15,000 Posts worldwide.

This marker indicates that the entombed was a member of the American Legion

Friendly Order of Eagles (FOE) and the Ladies Auxiliary

This club was started by a group of theater owners in Seattle in 1898. Originally called the Order of Good Things, it soon became known as the Fraternal Order of Eagles. Initially it was made up of actors, stagehands, playwrights, and theater owners. It grew to garner nationwide status, providing brotherhood, health benefits, and funeral and burial services.

Knights of Pythias (KP)

The Order of the Knights of Pythias is an international, non-sectarian fraternal order. This society was started in February of 1864 by Juastus H. Rathbone as a secret society for clerks employed by the federal government of the United States. Members pledge to promote understanding among men of good will as a way to attain universal peace; it is based on the maxim of Pythagoras, who said that the two most excellent things for man were to "speak the truth and render benefits to each other."

This person was a member of the Knights of Pythias

In the 1890s, there were close to 900,000 members, but recently that number has dropped to about 100,000. A heraldic shield and a suit of armor distinguish graves of members of this order. Sometimes the letters "F," "C," and "B" are found — they stand for friendship, charity, and benevolence.

Pythian Sisters (PS)

The female auxiliary of the Knights of Pythias was founded in 1888. Members are women over sixteen years old who speak English and believe in a Supreme Being. Their tombstones may have a Maltese cross with the letters "P," "L," "E," and "F" — they stand for purity, love, equality, and fidelity.

The Elks (BPOE)

The Benevolent Protective Order of Elks began as a club for actors known as "The Jolly Corks" in New York in 1866. It soon became a nationwide organization, changing its name around 1867 with the elk chosen as the symbol of the group.

This person belonged to the Elks.

Loyal Order of the Moose (LOOM)

Founded in 1888 by Dr. John Henry Wilson, this charitable group is known today as the Moose International. The group started with about 1,000 members, but this number had fallen to several hundred by the turn-of-the-century. James Davis, an early member of the LOOM, started selling insurance to members in 1906 with benefits being paid by the club to the members' surviving family. In the late 1920s, membership had risen to 650,000. Today there are over one and a half million members throughout the world.

Woodmen of the World (WOW)

Stones or markers in the shape of trees mark the members of this service organization that was founded in Nebraska in 1890 by Joseph Cullen Root. Sometimes the Latin phrase "Dum Tacet Clamet" is found; it means "though silent he speaks." It was originally open to members eighteen to forty-five years old who were in the woodworking profession.

Today there are 800,000 members. Until the 1920s, they provided each member with their own tombstone upon death under the adage that "no woodman ever lie in an unmarked grave." Some of the gravestones were made to resemble trees.

Trees mark the site of a Woodman of the World.

This marker also denotes a Woodman of the World.

An auxiliary for women was founded in Leadville, Colorado, and their headstones often have the words "courage," "hope," and "remembrance" on them.

Neighbors of Woodcraft (NOW)
In 1906, the Women of Woodcraft, Pacific Circle, relocated to Portland, Oregon and changed the name of their organization to reflect its acceptance of both male and female members. In 2001, the group merged with the Woodmen of the World and now have 7,000 members.

A marker with this symbol indicates that the woman was a Woman of Woodcraft.

Modern Woodmen of America (MWA)
This group is the fifth largest benevolent fraternal life insurance company around with over 750,000 members. They use the colors red to symbolize life and action, green to symbolize innocence and purity of intention, and white to symbolize immortality.

The Masons

The Masons, also known as Freemasons, are the oldest and largest fraternal organization in the world. Thirteen signers of the Constitution and fourteen US presidents belonged to this organization. The actual origins have been lost in time, but most scholars believe that Masonry rose from the guilds of stonemasons who had built the majestic castles of the Middle Ages. The organization was formalized in 1717 with the founding of the Grand Lodge. Masons believe in a Supreme Being and center their lives on their faith, are good citizens, and strive to make the world a better place. The Masons included such prestigious members

Masons showed their dedication with the Masonic symbol.

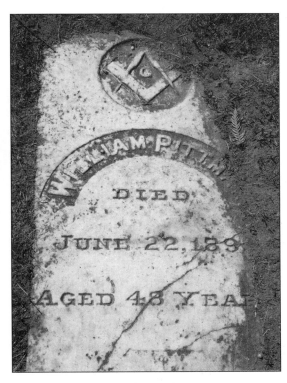

The Masons are an ancient order.

as Benjamin Franklin, Paul Revere, Alexander Hamilton, and George Washington.

The Shriners were an offshoot of the Masons in 1872. Originally they were only open to 32nd degree Masons. Their emblem is a scimitar blade with a five-pointed star and the motto "Robur et Furor" (Strength and Fury).

Commonly found on grave markers of the Masons are the compass and square as well as the all-seeing eye with rays of light coming out, which was an ancient symbol of God. Some of the letters that may be found in circles on Masons and Shiners' graves may be:

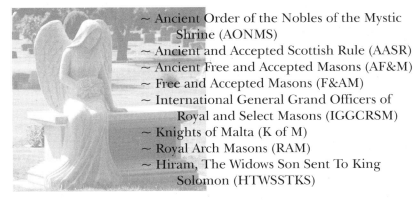

~ Ancient Order of the Nobles of the Mystic
    Shrine (AONMS)
~ Ancient and Accepted Scottish Rule (AASR)
~ Ancient Free and Accepted Masons (AF&M)
~ Free and Accepted Masons (F&AM)
~ International General Grand Officers of
    Royal and Select Masons (IGGCRSM)
~ Knights of Malta (K of M)
~ Royal Arch Masons (RAM)
~ Hiram, The Widows Son Sent To King
    Solomon (HTWSSTKS)

Knights Templar/Social Order of the Beauceant (KT and SOOB)

This group was founded in the year 1118 by a group of monastic warriors who had been charged with keeping the roads to Jerusalem safe for Pilgrims. The group grew into a wealthy organization and was considered so dangerous that in 1307 King Phillipe of France had them overthrown and took over their lands. The ladies' group was started in 1890 and is known as the Social Order of the Beauceant; Latin markings of "In Hoc Signo Vinces" translate to "In this sign shall you conquer."

Order of the Eastern Star/Prince Hall affiliated Easter Star (OES, PHES, ES, PHGCES)

Began in 1876, this was the female counterpart to the Masons. Graves of members have a five-pointed star with the tip pointing downwards and a letter at each point. The points are named after the women Adah, Ruth, Ester, Martha, and Electa. Sometimes the middle of each point will have the initials F, A, T, A, L, which symbolizes the oath the women took upon receipt of another degree.

The Order of the Eastern Star was the female counterpart of the Masons.

Eastern Star Past Matron

This symbol is founded on a tombstone as a five-pointed star with a link of chain and a suspended gavel, or a wreath of laurel circles circling the star with a gavel attached to the chair

Rainbow Girls/International Order of Rainbow Girls (RG/IORG)

This group was formed in 1922 for girls aged eleven to twenty as a counterpart to Demolay, which is for young men aged eleven to twenty. The letters "BFCL" are often found in a rainbow with a chain attached to a pot of gold and two clasped hands underneath signifying friendship. If the letter "R" is superimposed over the pot of gold, the person was a member of the International Order of the Rainbow for Girls.

Knights of the Maccabees (KOTM)

This group was almost wiped out by the Stock Market Crash of 1929, but was one of the more successful groups to be born out of the Civil War. The group takes its name from a second century Jewish tribe that was led in revolt by Judal Maccabeau against King Antiochus IV of Syria.

Ladies of the Macabees of the World (LOTM)

This fraternal benefit group was formed in 1892 and was the first to be run entirely by women. Tombstones usually have a beehive with a Latin inscription "ad astra per asperi," which translates to "towards the start through adversity."

Knights of Columbus (KC and K of C)

This fraternal organization for Catholics was started in 1882 after the Catholic Church barred its members from joining the Masons. Their symbol was adopted in 1883 and was designed by James T. Mullen, who was a Supreme Knight of the Order. The symbol appears as a medieval shield mounted on a former cross. Attached to the shield are fasces, which looks like a bundle of sticks wrapped together around an ax (a symbol of authority in Ancient Rome), an anchor to represent Columbus, and a short sword that was used on "errands of mercy" by Knights.

International Order of Odd Fellows (IOOF)

The Odd Fellows started in England in the eighteenth century as a benevolent and social club for men of the working class. The International Order of Odd Fellows is an offshoot from this organization. This society uses an All Seeing Eye as their emblem, along with two hands clasped in friendship beneath a three-link chain and the letters F, L, and T. The letters stand for Friendship, Love, and Truth. Behind the link on some stones are often found two battle-axes on long poles. Look for three linked rings.

Daughters of Rebecca (DR)

A female auxiliary of the Odd Fellows was started in 1851 and is considered to be subservient to the male order. A large number of members have dropped off, but their graves are marked with a crescent moon with seven stars to the right. The symbol also contains a dove (representing peace) and a white lily (representing purity).

Grand Army of the Republic (GAR)

This group is now extinct, but was open to discharged members of the Army, Navy, Marines, or Revenue Cutters who fought for the Union in the Civil War between April 12, 1861 and April 9, 1865. Founded shortly after the war by a surgeon named Benjamin Stephenson in Decatur, Illinois, the last encampment was held in 1949 and its last member (Albert Woolson) died in

Oddfellows mark their graves with three linking rings.

The Oddfellows are an ancient order that still exists today.

1956 at the age of 109. The group had 409,000 members in 1890, including five presidents. This made the group a powerful political organization for anyone who was seeking to run on the Republican ticket that needed an endorsement. Graves are identified by a five-pointed star medal with the tip pointing downwards and the letters GAR in the middle. A US flag with two crossed canons over a stack of cannonballs is above the five-pointed star.

Society of Mary (SM)

Found in certain areas of Catholic cemeteries, clergymen are often buried in what is known as a priests' circle. Two flowering vines surround a shield with the initials "MA" overlapped in the middle. Twelve stars representing the twelve founders of the school (congregation), which was created in 1836 by Fr. John Colin and eleven others who were attending seminary at the same time are placed above the shield. Beneath the shield is a banner with the phrase "Sub Mariae Nomine" (Under Mary's Name).

Companions of the Forest of America (CFA)

This English based group came to America in 1864. The Independent Order of Foresters broke off from the Royal Order in 1879 at the same time that the Catholic Order of Foresters was founded. The most successful group left is the International Order of Forester.

International Order of Red Men (IORM)

This group started before the Revolutionary War as the Sons of Liberty. After the war, they became the Society of Red Men with a reputation of being little more than a bunch of drunkards. Later the group reformed as the Improved Order of Red Men and in 1885 a women's auxiliary was formed called the Degree of Pocahontas. The grave marking of "T.O.T.E." stands for the Totem of the Eagle.

Salvation Army

William Booth formed this Christian organization as a quasi-military group in 1865 with the purpose of helping the needy and disadvantaged.

Fraternal Brotherhood (FB)

This group started as a secret beneficial society in 1896 and had considerable holdings, including a large building in Los Angeles that was featured on a 1910 postcard. The group may have been too secretive, as it no longer exists.

Independent Order of B'nai B'rith (IOBB)

The Children of the Covenant was started in New York in 1843 because Jews were not allowed in any of the other clubs. It is also known as the Anti-Defamation League. In Jewish cemeteries or in Jewish sections of cemeteries, the gravestone may be marked with the initials "IOBB."

Chapter Six:

Seattle's Creepy Cemeteries... & Beyond

People are fascinated with the final resting spots of celebrities. Since ghost hunters spend a lot of time in these areas, they get to know the "lay of the land." Seattle ghost hunters are often asked, "Where is Jimmi Hendrix buried?" (Renton) or "Where are Bruce and Brandon Lee?" (Lakeview) Sometimes they are given a challenge, such as, "What cemetery holds Kurt Cobain?" (None... He was cremated and his ashes were sprinkled at sea.)

This section provides some information about cemeteries found in the Seattle area that explorers can check out on their own. Historical records are fragile and, while some information may be obtained from headstones, researchers should check out old newspaper accounts and online sources such as Historylink.org to find out what was happening during the era when these people were interred.

Public libraries can point people in the right direction as well. The Everett Public Library has an iPod tour online that may be downloaded as an MP3 file and provides a walking tour of the Evergreen Cemetery (www.epls.org/nw/).

Comet Lodge Cemetery

This cemetery was disputed for many years, as King County officials claimed it was not a cemetery and wanted to turn it into a park for dogs, despite the tombstones that were still located there. The cross streets for this cemetery is South Graham Street and 23rd Avenue South. The county had expressed their intention to restore the cemetery "with sensitivity, dignity, and integrity." Today dogs are allowed to run through the unfenced property.

The site was originally used by the Duwamish nation. When the Maple family settled the area, they referred to the cemetery area as the Old Burial Grounds. There were many Duwamish members recorded on the Tribal roll buried there before the family arrived and as many as eight hundred pioneers may have been buried here over time as well. The Maple family settled in the area and lived peacefully alongside the Duwamish Tribe. The Maple family then deeded the land to the IOOF Comet Lodge, which platted, dedicated, and recorded the land, establishing the cemetery in 1895.

While the grounds were somewhat abandoned in the 1920s, the remains of deceased people were added to this hallowed ground until 1930 when other cemeteries became popular. The last recorded burial was that of a three-year-old child named Jewel Lundin, who passed away September 21, 1936.

The Comet Lodge Cemetery eventually became neglected and overgrown with brambles. While cemeteries are protected sites, ownership of this particular land came into question and the city of Seattle and King County had several rounds of foreclosure actions. Many civic groups have attempted to protect the graveyard through the years.

In 1959, a past Lodge member sent a letter to the County detailing a plan to move the cemetery, stating that the cost of moving the bodies would be recovered by the sale of the land. Nothing was

Comet Lodge Cemetery… A burial ground? A dog park? A haunted story?

done and years later the City would officially declare that there had never been a cemetery at that location!

Property lines seem to have become blurred in this area. In the 1970s, houses were built over parts of the cemetery where children had been buried. The City assured homeowners that there was not a graveyard on Beacon Hill. There are ten or twelve houses that were built on this "baby land." An article from the Seattle Times in 1985 reported that "…nobody knows the exact boundaries and nobody is certain where the bodies are situated because the detailed map has been mislaid and most gravestones have disappeared." This information can be verified by checking a copy of Volume 9 of Plats and looking on page 19 from King County. Indeed, many people have reported that they found gravestones from the cemetery in various places.

One person reported that their father told them they found a gravestone that had been stolen and dumped in the alley behind their house. In 1965, members of a small garage band (who wish to remain anonymous) stole a gravestone from the cemetery and took it to the basement where they practiced and would burn candles on top of it during their rehearsals. This stone marked the location of Cynthia Brownlee, who was born in 1833. County records show that she died June 26, 1898 and was buried in the Comet Lodge Cemetery at the age of sixty-eight. Cynthia would have seen the city of Seattle rise up and be burned down in the great fire. She would have seen the rebirth of the city... One wonders how her spirit took to the Seattle music scene as the band played on in their basement. Eventually one of the band members convinced the rest of them to return the stone to the cemetery. Not knowing where they originally took it from, they abandoned it along the edge of the cemetery.

One family had an expensive collection of porcelain dolls that they kept on display in an illuminated cabinet. They kept the cabinet locked and checked the lock nightly. Despite this security measure, the owner would find the dolls scattered around the house the next morning as if some ghostly spirit had been playing with the dolls.

Another family criticized their only son for leaving his toys around the house all the time. The boy protested and claimed that he was not playing with the toys, but was forced by his parents to clean up his room before going to bed each night. He dutifully placed the toys in a box each night, but the next morning the toys were discovered all over the house. They were found on the stairs and on every level of the home. Finally, the child confided to his parents that a strange boy, dressed in funny clothes, came into his room each night and sat on the edge of the bed. The boy felt that the spirit was watching over him.

One of the homeowners told reporters that she was assured that her property was not part of the Comet Lodge Cemetery, but felt that they were not alone from the start. The day that they moved in, all the lights suddenly went out and then came on all by themselves. She told the reporter that they knew the spirits were there and they live with it. Several times she turned off the lights in her display case, left the room, and came back to find the lights on again. Suspecting that her children were playing a trick on her, she turned the lights off one time and went to her bedroom. She stood at the door to spy on the case and the lights came back on...all by themselves! One night while she was making dinner, she saw a clear cloud swoop past her. She followed the ghost to her bedroom, where she saw it more clearly — a full outline of a person — as if in a cloud. The spirit then swooped into the bathroom.

Her daughter also says that she has seen spirits. One day she visited the cemetery and then came home to her bedroom. When she looked out her bedroom window, she saw a ghost. This spectral woman had long hair with lose waves and approached the little girl's window. The spirit looked happy so she got up and looked at her. Other children reported that they have seen ghosts as well. People have reported seeing strange lights and actual apparitions in the cemetery at night. Many of the reports indicate that the spirits are short, probably children, that run and dart between the trees. Psychics claim that there are probably between fifty and one hundred spirits hanging around the area.

In 1987, a Beacon Hill Resident Don Kipper began to clear off the land after acquiring clear title to the property from two of the three Lodge owners. It soon became apparent that he really intended to build his home there. Apparently he had a lifelong dream to live on a cemetery! Yet people thought he was restoring it. During the same period, the City of Seattle began a sewer line project through the cemetery!

Although Kipper lacked any rights or finances to restore its grounds, he managed to convince city workers to bulldoze the tombstones on All Souls Day, November 2, 1987. They were there deeply trenching the sacred grounds putting in a sewer main! A restraining order was enacted to "safeguard the cemetery," although the city took no action to prevent further desecration and completed the sewer project. Shortly after the incident, the city changed the zones of this area from cemetery to single family residence and retail space, thereby making it official that there was no cemetery on Beacon Hill.

This resulted in an ownership challenge over the cemetery that lasted another decade! John Dickinson took the project under his wing as the subject of his Master's study at Seattle University. John's cousin found the gravestone of their great-great grandfather (who had been the last mayor of Southpark) as well as that of their great-grandfather. John had a work permit issued by the County, good for five years, and a promise that the cemetery would be turned over to his non-profit organization. He began to work on restoring the property.

Emotions ran high as John sought to protect and restore the cemetery with his non-profit organization at no expense to the taxpayers. One objection to these honorable activities came from a city employee who had reportedly been seen removing grave markers from the cemetery. It seems that this person wanted to protect her source of markers and eventually managed to get John barred from the cemetery by claiming that a protected species (the red-tailed hawk) was being disturbed by the non-profit restoration activities.

Eventually the county gave up on its promised, but costly plan to restore the cemetery with "sensitivity, dignity, and integrity" and completed its plan to turn it into a dog-run park, investing over $100,000 to give the park a cemetery appearance. There remain some wonderful examples of gravestone markers from the Woodmen of the World, but as one walks the cemetery it seems apparent that there is no pattern, rhyme, or reason for the placement of the handful of stones. According to King County records, there are 494 people buried in the cemetery!

In 2006, I spoke with John, who said that some of the wooden cross baby markers were stored in a tavern for a while and others were taken from the site by residents who wanted to use them in their gardens after being told that the cemetery was abandoned. Two avenues — 22nd and 23rd — now encroaches on the cemetery and in the middle of that avenue one can find marks where the asphalt was melted to find the survey markers for the cemetery when Mr. Dickinson had the site surveyed. Web resources for future investigations on the Comet Lodge Cemetery complete with photos, maps, and drawings can be found at:

~ http://worldperc.com/comet/faqs.html
~ http://dailyuw.com/2008/10/31/ghosts-comet-lodge-cemetery
~ www.interment.net/data/us/wa/king/comet_lodge.html

DENNY PARK

This scenic little park was Seattle's first city cemetery. Bodies were prepared at Butterworth's Mortuary and viewed at their chapel on 2nd Street before being moved to the cemetery on Denny Street. Visitors today can follow the route of the dearly departed by stopping at Kells Pub in Pike Market, which is the current site of the former mortuary. The body was then taken out the back door to the chapel on Second Street — it's now the Starlite Lounge, where the entranceway still has tiles on the floor that read "Chapel" and "Office."

As the city grew, it was decided that the bodies should be moved to the new Lakeview Cemetery. As part of the process of leveling out the terrain in Seattle, known as the Denny Regrade, the city used high-pressure hoses to lower high land sites, and this cemetery lost sixty feet of its altitude. During the process of moving the bodies, citizens complained that the bodies should not be dragged through the city during the day, so workers were instructed to do so at night — thus the phrase "graveyard shift" was born!

GRAND ARMY OF THE REPUBLIC

This small cemetery is found at 1200 West Howe Street at Everett Avenue E and East Howe Street. It has soldiers of the Civil War interred there next to the larger, more popular Lakeview Cemetery. Observers have reported seeing ghosts in Civil War uniforms walking through the area. The cemetery closes at 11:30 p.m.

(Author's note: Of personal interest to me, a "Teeple" is buried there! I always find it strange to go through a cemetery and find my name on a marker!)

GREENWOOD MEMORIAL PARK CEMETERY

This cemetery is located at 350 Monroe NE, in the Highlands area of Renton, and is the final resting place of Jimmi Hendrix. It is well-kept and maintained with beautiful statuary and a very nice Asian section. Of particular note is the monument dedicated to Jimmi Hendrix — visitors from around the world come to do gravestone rubbings of the monument and leave tokens of respect for the musician.

HILL GROVE CEMETERY

Established in 1900, this site is near the Seattle-Tacoma Airport at 200th Street and Des Moines Way South. Since its founding, the property has been surrounded by the airport. It also suffers from poor maintenance and vandalism.

MALTBY CEMETERY

There have been a lot of words written about the haunted cemetery in Maltby. Legend has it that it was established by a satanic family as a final resting place and that in the middle of the cemetery there are thirteen steps that lead to nowhere. If people walk down the steps…they perish instantly! Or go directly to Hell (don't pass go and don't even see $200)…or they see their spirit in hell… Reportedly, one man ran across the cemetery, was frightened, and was never seen again!

The Washington Ghost Hunters Society claim that when investigators walk around the gravestones and turn to come back…one of the headstones turns into a magnificent marker and the wind whispers. Occasionally a woman has been seen searching for a child.

Reports persist of a guard ghost that protects the area and provides a warning to people that if they enter a certain area they will lose their minds. Other visitors have reported hearing the sound of horses' hooves and rumor has it that there may be the ghost of a mounted watchman who roams the area.

Officially listed on maps as the Paradise Valley Cemetery, the biggest mystery seems to be finding it! The Evergreen Paranormal website directs searchers to the Redmond/Duvall Road, where there are about fifteen gravesites. They report that women and children have been seen in old raggedy clothes wandering around the graves.

In September 2006, I was in the area and decided to find the place. The map coordinates (for those of you who like to use GoogleEarth) are: Lat: 47° 46° 33°N, 122° 04° 46°W (T26N R6E Sec 6). It can be difficult to find since there is no Redmond/Duvall Road and no signs directing you to the cemetery. Furthermore, it's actually in Woodinville! However, someone is currently using and maintaining the cemetery. (Demons on John Deere tractors? Or perhaps benevolent neighbors.) To get there:

> Take I-405 North towards Monroe. At the Maltby cutoff, take Paradise Lake Road south. Once you pass back into King County (there's a sign), be ready to turn right onto 202nd Avenue NE (Reintree Country Estates). Take the next left, which is unmarked, but is 203rd Place and ends in a cul-de-sac. You'll see the no trespassing signs right in front of you.

The property is unimpressive and surrounded by expensive houses, whose owners have probably thought of the land as an extension of their homes since 1989. It is marked as private property with no trespassing signs posted at the entrance. I can understand the local people wanting to keep the cemetery a secret. The house on the left as you enter the site is valued at over $850,000. This may account for the "angry local farmer who chased people out of the cemetery." However, there is no ownership identification that you may use to gain permission to enter, and the single eroded log across the entranceway is easily stepped over. Remember that the land is posted and you should always get permission before entering this type of location.

The site is located on terraced property, with the headstones on lovely terraced lanes that loved ones can walk along. I did not find a den of any sort, no steps other than the terraced landscape, nor any satanic markings on the headstones. One headstone did surprise me when I walked passed it the second time, since I had not noticed it the first time, which may account for the legend of the grave marker that turns into a magnificent monument. The terraced land goes down into undeveloped terrain that leads to the roadway — I suppose that anyone going down thirteen undeveloped terraces would burst out into the roadway (197th Avenue NE) and encounter a lumber truck speeding along the county road...speedily dispatching the investigator to their own version of heaven or hell. During my visit I took lots of pictures and readings, but there were no orbs or anomalies...at least, not at 3 o'clock in the afternoon. Perhaps, as the surrounding land was developed, one of the houses may have been built over the thirteen steps...

MOUNT OLIVET CEMETERY

This picturesque private cemetery is located in Renton about two miles north of Greenwood Memorial Park. Chief William of the Duwamish Tribe was buried there in 1896. There have been reported lights in the area, a stone ball that seems to move on its own volition, and even a fairy ring! One set of investigators was looking for signs of spirits and a worker asked them what they were doing, then laughed, and said, "I know what you are looking for...you want to know where the fairy ring is!"

MOUNT PLEASANT CEMETERY

This forty-acre cemetery is located on the north side of Queen Ann Hill at 700 West Raye Street. This is the final resting place of some of the unclaimed bodies from the 1910 Wellington Train Disaster from Stevens Pass.

NEWCASTLE CEMETERY

This site was established in 1879 as the final resting place for coal miners who produced twenty-two percent of the coal shipped from the Pacific Coast. This cemetery is one of the few reminders of the area's mining history, the miners, and their families. It is located south of 69th Way, off 129th Avenue SE in the town of Newcastle.

Chapter Seven:

LAKEVIEW CEMETERY

This is the land where all those bodies that were moved from Denny Park ended up. One man, to the dismay of his neighbors, buried his horse in Lakeview Cemetery. The townsfolk demanded that he remove the horse, and the man agreed, but he only removed the headstone. He left the body of the horse in the cemetery. This may account for the sightings of a white luminous horse that has been seen grazing among the tombstones.

Martial arts expert and movie star Bruce Lee is buried at Lakeview Cemetery at the north side of Volunteer Park (1554 15th Avenue East). His son, Brandon, lies next to him. At their gravesite, compasses have been known to act erratically, with ghost hunters recording EVPs on a regular basis.

Who's Who at Lakeview

Many of Seattle's founders are buried at Lakeview Cemetery on the north side of Volunteer Park. The people listed in this section all lived in the 1850s. They most likely new each other and had dealings with each other. The cemetery is their final resting place, where we honor those who have come before us.

As you read about the following pioneers, remember that they are presented here so that you can consider how they all interacted with each other when they were alive. Imagine Arthur Denny bumping into Mrs. Maynard on a summer's day outside the Yesler sawmill. What did they discuss, who else did they know, and how did they react when Madam Conklin came up the street? They all knew each other; they had their lives, laughs, and loves—and now all rest together on a hill overlooking the city that they built.

Henry Allen Atkins, 1827-1885
Elected the first Mayor of Seattle, Henry served from 1869 to 1871. During its first incorporation, the city tended to operate as a personal fiefdom, run by the most prominent founders. Henry ran a mercantile business in Seattle's first brick building. He also served as sheriff in an attempt to bring order to the growing town.

Carson D. Boren, 1824-1912

An early pioneer, Carson was part of the Denny expedition that arrived November 13, 1851 at Alki Beach. He built the first cabin in the present city of downtown Seattle at the corner of Second Avenue and Cherry Street, the current site of the Hoge Building.

Carson was the brother of Louisa Boren Denny. His original claim included waterfront property. While he was out of town in Olympia getting livestock, his brother-in-law, Arthur Denny, gave that land to Henry Yesler to build a sawmill. When Carson returned, he found that he no longer owned waterfront property as his brother-in-law had simply moved Carson's claim stakes!

Arthur Armstrong Denny, 1822-1899

Founder of Seattle, Arthur was the leader of the pioneer Denny party that landed at Alki Point November 13, 1851. He was also a key land donor and founder of the University of Washington in 1861 and a Territorial delegate to Congress from 1865 to 1867. Arthur was the older brother of David T. Denny and brother-in-law of Carson Boren.

Milton Holgate, 1840-1856

This Seattle youth was killed during the one significant Indian attack known as the Battle of Seattle. He was killed looking out the door of the Felker Hotel, which was managed by Madam Conklin. This son of John C. Holgate, a Duwamish pioneer, was an innocent bystander, just wanting to see what was happening. Holgate Street is named after him and is passed by thousands of commuters each day who travel the I-5 expressway into the city from the south.

Mary Ann Conklin, died in 1873...or 1887

Seattle's first hotel, the Felker House, was built on 1st Avenue and Main Street. It was run by Mary Ann Conklin, who later added a brothel to the top floor. She was known for her nasty disposition and an absolutely filthy mouth that she used to sear in no less than five languages! Her hotel burned to the ground in the Great Fire of 1889.

Mary Ann reportedly passed away in 1873. She was buried in Lakeview Cemetery beneath a simple stone that attests to her personality in life. The original stone read: "Mother Damnable Conklin" with the year of her death listed as 1887. In 2007, the old gravestone was replaced with a more suitable stone and corrected her date of death as 1873. Even in death, it seems, someone is lying about their age...

Her final resting spot is the third one she's been in, having been moved twice! One can find the headstone by looking for the sunken roadway that used to lead up the hill along the cemetery. In 1886, she was moved from Washelli Cemetery to the current site. The gravediggers did not want to carry her heavy coffin any further than they had to, so

Mother Damnable Conklin's gravestone.

when the wagon stopped, they planted Mary next to the old roadway. Look for the signs of the old rutted road next to her gravesite.

David S. Maynard, 1808-1873

"Doc Maynard" was a prominent Pioneer Seattle doctor who managed to name the City of Seattle after Chief Sealth. He was the territory Indian Agent and helped create the Washington Territory. He was the first to be buried in Lakeview Cemetery, at the highest point on Seattle's Capitol Hill.

Catherine Troutman Maynard, 1816-1906

One of the founders of Seattle and wife of Dr. David S. Maynard, Catherine was the last survivor of an 1850 Oregon wagon train party stricken with cholera in Wyoming. Doc Maynard stopped to help and later married the widow. She is buried at the highest point in Lakeview Cemetery, which is the highest point in Seattle, alongside her husband. Her epitaph reads: "She did what she could."

Thomas Mercer, 1813-1898

This Seattle pioneer was captain of a wagon train that arrived in Seattle in 1853. He named Lake Washington and Lake Union. Mercer Island, Washington, is named for him. His younger brother was Asa Mercer, who brought a shipment of "brides" to frontier Seattle.

William Renton, 1818-1891

Founder of Renton Coal Company and the city of Renton, Washington, William came to Seattle from San Francisco in 1852, eventually setting up a business on Blakely Harbor on Bainbridge Island. He invested heavily in the coal trade. The city of Renton is named after him.

Corliss Stone, 1838-1906

He was elected the third Mayor of Seattle in 1872, serving only seven months in office. In 1873, he was involved in a major political scandal and accused of embezzling $15,000 ($550,000 in present day dollars) from a real estate development firm of which he was a principal investor. He fled down the Pacific Coast, arriving in San Francisco in the company of a married woman.

Prior to being elected Mayor, Stone also served three one-year terms on the town council from 1869 to 1872 and was instrumental in the creation of Seattle's first Chamber of Commerce. He was also active in the development of residential property, plotting the current Seattle neighborhoods of Wallingford and Fremont, and was active in the social community. In 1872, he was appointed director of the Library Association and served as a trustee of the Plymouth Congregational Society. Two major street arterials, Stone Way and Corliss Avenue located in Seattle's Wallingford community, still remain today in the former mayor's honor.

Henry L. Yesler, 1830 - 1892

Mayor of Seattle from 1874 to 1875 and 1885 to 1886, Henry operated Yesler's Sawmill, the first steam-powered sawmill in Puget Sound, fed by the original "Skid Road." The land was donated to him by Doc Maynard and Carson Boren, who thought the sawmill would produce revenue and job opportunities in the newfound city. Henry ultimately made his fortune in real estate and, in 1875, he sold a lot of land (24 x 70 feet) at what is now 1st Avenue and Yesler Way for $6,000. The new owners sold the land in 1889 for $19,000, an increase in value of $13,000 in fourteen years. The Seattle Real Estate Bubble had begun!

Another source of income for Yesler was the first lottery that was held in Washington on July 4, 1876. The Grand Lottery of Washington was advertised by Yesler, who raised about $30,000 ($1.3 million in today's dollars). At the last minute, Yesler cancelled the drawing and kept about ninety percent of the money. For his fraud, he was assessed a fine of $25 (about $1,000 in today's dollars).

Angels are often used as sites of comfort, indicating that the deceased has been guided to a better place.

Section Three:
HAUNTED TOURS AND WEBSITES

Chapter Eight:

WHERE TO FIND THE GHOSTS

GHASTLY GHOST TOURS

For the new ghost hunter, there is a wealth of information to obtain about a city or haunted area by taking a ghost tour. These tours are organized by knowledgeable people who have spent considerable amounts of time researching the interesting stories behind the hauntings. Some of the tours are walking tours, while other tours include transportation of some type. Ghost tours can be found nationwide by using the Internet search engine and typing in "ghost tours." They are sometimes called ghost walks, haunted tours, walking tours, or other creative names. These expeditions can be found in most large cities such as Tombstone, Washington, DC, and Gettysburg. Even Paris, France has a walking tour of their underground tombs, where millions of Parisians are entombed; spectators walk right next to the stacked bones of the deceased French!

To participate in a tour, investigators usually make a reservation in advance and the operator will advise the person where to meet the tour guide. Cameras, tape recorders, and other types of equipment are normally welcome on the tours as long as they do not interfere with the tour itself. These tours are very popular among tourists to the city. Dress appropriately for the tour with good walking shoes and perhaps a jacket, umbrella, and flashlight. Some tours meet in the daylight and then move to more remote locations that may become dark, damp, and slippery, and involve climbing old ladders and stairs. Tours tend to last about ninety minutes to two hours.

At the tour site, the group is met by their guide. Groups are normally small and consist of not more than a dozen people. Since this is a guided tour, all people have to be able to hear the guide's explanation of what is happening and going on. The guides often dress to act the part. Some dress in turn-of-the-century Victorian garb, others as funeral directors, and some even as vampires or gothic characters with flowing capes, top hats, and canes. It's all part of the entertainment package and these guides have a penchant for the theatrical. Don't be afraid to ask them to pose with you for a photo or two!

After the group is advised of the safety precautions to be taken during the tour, the guide will spirit the group away to their first stop. Along the way, the guide will present historical information about the tour, the city, and the area that they are going to. Upon arrival at the first stop, the guide will present the assembled group with the story of the building, any ghost reports of the area, rumors, legends, and other tidbits of information. The group is given a short amount of time to explore the immediate area, take photographs, and sound recordings before being ushered to the next area by the tour guide. "Everyone move along, stay together, we're walking, we're walking, we're stalking…"

Ghost tours are led by guides who take care to ensure the safety of the group as well as to share some of the little known history of the area. Colorful anecdotes of the normal and not so normal people who make up a thriving metropolis add to the fun and excitement of a ghost tour. While there is no guarantee that ghosts will be encountered, participants often come away with tales of "something unusual" that happened on that tour. For this reason ghost hunters often carry their equipment with them in search of EVPs or other indications of a haunting. Since ghost tours are limited to a number of people on each tour, advance reservations are recommended.

A following is a listing of local tours in the area:

Pike Market Ghost Tour

A light walking tour usually conducted around Halloween by shop owners in the Pike Market, the tour highlights the history of Pike Market with some ghost stories mixed in to make a fun excursion for tourists. The tours last about an hour and costs $15. Contact Mercedes at 206-322-1218 to arrange a guided tour of this landmark! (www.marketghost.com)

The Museum of the Mysteries

This tour is dedicated to the exploration of the weird and wonderful. Topics range from Bigfoot to UFOs to ghosts and they have an extensive research library. Their Capitol Hill Ghost Tour is part history, part ghost tales, and entirely entertaining!

Charlette LeFevre and Phillip Lipson are two of the most informed people about the mysteries that haunt the Seattle area. The museum itself is in the Deluxe Building at 623 Broadway East. The ghost tours last about one hour and depart from the Museum of the Mysteries each Saturday at 5 and 7 p.m. There is a suggested donation of $5 for the tour. If you can't make the tour, stop by and explore the museum, which is also haunted!

The Seattle Underground Tour

Participants are guided into parts of the city that are normally not seen. (Portland, Oregon, also has a tour of this type.) This type of tour is a bit more energetic as the tourists get to climb through old abandoned areas, explore history, and learn of some of the more seedy parts of town and some of the ghostly activities that tend to happen there.

Tourists gather at a central location such as Doc Maynard's in Seattle, where they meet their guide, who will explain how Pioneer Square has an entertaining history of plumbing catastrophes, scandals, and misadventures. This year-round tour takes about ninety minutes and costs around $14, which must be paid in cash, and is first come/first served. For more information, call 206-682-4646 or check them out on the Internet at www.undergroundtour.com.

Private Eye Tours

This is an escorted tour with transportation provided. In Seattle, tourists can be escorted in a van by Jake of Private Eye Tours. Jake picks up participants at hotels or restaurants and chauffeurs them to the sites. The tour involves minimal walking and is available throughout the year. The tour takes about two and a half to three hours and costs about $25. For more information, contact Jake directly at 206-365-3739 or visit his website at www.privateeyetours.com.

Portland Walking Tours

They offer a "Beyond Bizarre" tour, where people on the tour are given electromagnetic field meters (EMF) to detect the spirits. The tour takes visitors through the Merchant Hotel at Northwest Davis and Second streets, which is now the location of Olde Town Pizza. They only allow twenty people and the tours often sell out. Be sure to buy tickets in advance at 503-774-4522. The 10 p.m. tour on Friday and Saturday costs $29 and includes a voucher for a drink at the bar. The tour lasts about two and a half hours. Meet at the Olde Town Pizza at 226 NW Davis Street.

Chapter Nine:

The Web's Haunted Resources

Like peeling an onion, ghost hunting leads to layer after layer of interesting material. The Internet is a valuable resource and most ghost hunting organizations have photos and links to other sites for further research. Some of the basic sites are listed here.

† Amateur Ghost Hunters of Seattle/Tacoma: www.aghost.com
† International Ghost Hunters Society: www.ghostweb.com
† Organization of Ghosts and Hauntings Research Society: www.ghrs.org
† American Association Electronic Voice Phenomena: www.aaevp.com
† Pike Market Ghost Tours: www.marketghost.com
† Seattle Ghost Tours by Jake: www.privateeyetours.com

Other Websites of Interest

† www.ghostpix.com: Has examples of EVPs and ghost photography.
† www.ghost-voices.com and www.evpvoices.com: Both sites have a large collection of EVPs.
† www.ghostvillage.com and www.seattleghosthunters.com: Has examples of ghost research.
† www.americanghosts.com, www.theshadowlands.net, and www.ghostandcritters.com: These websites offer a complete listing of haunted locations.
† www.zerotime.com and www.riptx.dns2go.com: These sites contain information on the paranormal and paranormal photos that can be viewed.
† www.magickmind.net: Features a paranormal talk radio show.
† www.hauntster.net: This website features anomalies with attitude.
† www.ghostmag.com: A ghost magazine website.
† www.hollowhill.com: This site contains images and information on Fort Worden.

Video available on the Internet

† The Wah Mee Massacre: You Tube at http://post.thestranger.com/seattle/Video?show=297560
† Harvard Exit Ghost video: This feature originally appeared on CityStream 10/25/2007, the Seattle Channel's weekly magazine show. Go to http://www.seattlechannel.org/videos/video.asp?ID=30707292
† Pike Place Market Centennial Celebration: Ghost Stories first aired on August 16, 2007. Go to http://www.seattlechannel.org/videos/video.asp?ID=4030739.

Websites by State

Alabama: Mystical Blaze (www.mysticalblaze.com)
Alaska: Paranormal Photos.com (http://paranormalphotos.tripod.com)
Arizona: Arizona Paranormal Investigations (www.arizonaparanormalinvestigations.
    com)
Arkansas: The Spirit Seekers (www.thespiritseekers.org)
California: Ghost Trackers (www.ghost-trackers.org)
Colorado: All About Ghosts (www.allaboutghosts.com)
Connecticut: Ghosthound (www.ghosthound.com)
Delaware: Paranormal Investigations (http://pages.zdnet.com/dprs/ghosts/)
Florida: GHG Ghost Hunters (www.ghgghosthunters.com)
Georgia: Ghost Force (www.ghostforce.com)
Hawaii: Kwaiden (www.geocities.com/Area51/Hollow/6166)
Idaho: Idaho Spirit Seekers (www.geocities.com/idahospiritseekers/index.html)
Illinois: Ghost Research Society (www.ghostresearch.org)
Indiana: Shadowchasers of NWI (www.nwishadowchasers.homestead.com)
Kansas: Seekers of the Unknown (www.seekersoftheunknown.homestead.com)
Kentucky: Southern Paranormal Research (www.southernghostresearch.org)
Louisiana: The Haunted Traveler (www.hauntedtraveler.com)
Maryland: Ghost & Spirit Assocociation (www.marylandghosts.com)
Massachusetts: Cape and Island Association (www.caiprs.com)
Michigan: Mid Michigan Ghost Hunter Society (www.mmghs.com)
Missouri: Missouri Ghost Hunter Society (www.ghosthaunting.com)
Nebraska: Grasping Shadows (www.geocities.com/graspingshadows)
Nevada: NV Ghosts & Hauntings (www.ghrs.org/nevada/)
New Jersey: South Jersey Ghost Research (http/southjerseyghostresearch.org)
New York: NY Ghost Chapter (www.newyorkghostchapter.com)
North Carolina: L.E.M.U.R. (www.phantoms.cc)
Ohio: Ohio Paranormal (www.angelfire.com/oh3/opin)
Oklahoma: OK Ghost Patrol (http://okghostpatrol.net)
Oregon: Pacific Paranormal (www.nwpprs.com)
Pennsylvania: Cathes Ghost Encounters (http://hauntedfieldsofglory.com)
Rhode Island: T.A.P.S. (http://the-atlantic-paranormal-society.com)
South Carolina: Coastal Spirit Chasers (www.coastalspiritchasers.net)
Tennessee: Ghosts of Tennessee (www.tnghost.org)
Texas: Ghastly Ghost Hunter (www.ghastlyghosthunter.com)
Utah: Utah Ghost Organization (www.utahghost.org)
Virginia: Spheres of Influence (www.carfaxabbey.net/spheres)
Washington: SeattleTacoma Ghost Hunt (www.aghost.us); Washington State PIR
    (www.wspir.com); Jefferson Davis (www.ghostsandcritters.com)
West Virginia: WV Society of Ghost Hunt (www.wvsocietyofghosthunters.com)
Wisconsin: SW Paranormal Research (www.paranormalresearchgroup.homestead.
    com)

BIBLIOGRAPHY

Auerbach, Lloyd. *How to Investigate the Paranormal*. Berkely, California: Ronin Publishing, 2004.

Bragg, L. E. *Myths and Mysteries of Washington*. Guilford, Connecticut: Globe Pequot Press, 2005.

Davis, Jeff. *Ghosts, Critters, & Sacred Places II*. Winfield, Kansas: Central Plains Book Mfg., 2000.

Ghosts, Critters, & Sacred Places III. Winfield, Kansas: Central Plains Book Mfg., 2005.

Dwyer, Jeff. *Ghost Hunter's Guide to Seattle and Puget Sound*. Gretna, Louisiana: Pelican Publication, 2008.

Emerson, Jim. "Ghost Stories: Haunted Movie Houses." *Pacific Northwest*. Seattle, Washington: Department of Development brochure, 1985.

Glenday, Craig. *The UFO Investigator's Handbook*. Philadelphia, Pennsylvania: Running Press, 1999.

Keister, Douglas. *Stories in Stone*. Layton, Utah: Gibbs Smith, 2003.

Krist, Gary. *The White Cascade*. New York, New York: Henry Holt, 2007.

Lind, Carol. "Haunted Brothel." *Western Gothic*. Seattle, Washingon: Lind, 1983.

Smith, Barbara. *Ghost Stories of Washington*. Renton, Washington: Lone Pine Publishing, 2000.

Southall, Richard. *How to be a Ghost Hunter*. St. Paul, Minnesota: Llewellyn Publications, 2003.

Speidel, William. *Sons of the Profits*. Seattle, Washington: Nettle Creek, 1967.

Teeples, Allison. *Ghostology 101*. Indianapolis, Indiana: Authorhouse, 2005.

Warren, Joshua P. *How to Hunt Ghosts: A Practical Guide*. New York, New York: Simon and Shuster, 2003.

Willbanks, Athena. *Ghosts of Seattle*. Atglen, Pennsylvania: Schiffer Publishing, Ltd., 2007.